ENCORE

A HIGH ACHIEVER'S GUIDE TO THRIVING IN RETIREMENT

ELIZABETH ZELINKA PARSONS

Editing, design, distribution by Bublish
Published by Zelinka Parsons Publications

ISBN: 979-8-9901694-1-8 (paperback)
ISBN: 979-8-9901694-0-1 (hardcover)
ISBN: 979-8-9901694-2-5 (eBook)

DEDICATION

This book is dedicated to my Sunday Dinner crew for giving me many of the best evenings of my life. You know who you are.

CONTENTS

PART TWO
IDENTITY CRISIS: WHO WILL I BE IF I'M NOT WHAT I DO?

PART THREE
RETHINKING LIFE'S ARCHITECTURE: DESIGN GUIDELINES FOR THE FORMERLY HECTIC PROFESSIONAL

PART FOUR
MAKING IT REAL: GETTING STARTED, CHARTING
PROGRESS, AND ENJOYING THE RIDE

AUTHOR'S NOTE

Throughout this book, I have drawn heavily from the stories of clients who have attended our Encore Program, which was created to help high-achieving professionals design a purposeful and energizing plan for their next chapters. Unless I have used our clients' full names with their express permission, I have changed names, specific contextual facts, and other identifying characteristics in order to protect privacy and ensure confidentiality. I am deeply grateful to them all for placing their trust in me and for the lessons that come out of their experiences. My hope is that the lessons shared in this book help many others as they approach and navigate the monumental inflection point known as "retirement."

INTRODUCTION

I have always been a high-achiever type. I have a vivid memory of sitting at an awards ceremony in fourth grade, and as the fifth grader on stage was accepting her prize for the best grades in the school that year, I vowed to myself it would be me up there the next year. From that day on, I placed a death grip on achievement and insisted I perform at the peak of excellence, no matter what the endeavor or circumstances. I took top marks as the valedictorian of my high school graduating class and then graduated summa cum laude from undergrad with two majors and a minor. When I pursued my law degree at Georgetown University Law Center, I did so in the night program while working full time during the day, graduating magna cum laude. You get the idea, yes?

When hard work and good fortune conspired to land me at one of the world's top international law firms, I took it no less seriously. I thrust myself into working life fully, determined to be the absolute best law firm associate I could be. But now that no one was passing out grades, I found it harder and harder to know if I was acing it. *No problem*, I figured. *As long as I just work as hard as humanly possible, I'll be mostly assured of my right to be here.*

And so, I did that. For the better part of a decade.

Meanwhile, by age thirty-two, I had gotten married and become a mother, new roles I promptly decided I could also ace. Just find another gear; learn more things; focus on efficiency; be a better human; get by on less sleep. As my responsibilities at the firm continued to expand, as my family life continued to offer me more and more to care about, and as my second child entered this world, I found the end of my capacity to "just work harder." I had heartbreakingly (and also thankfully) finally hit the wall. Feeling defeated, I believed I was failing at everything that mattered, including career and motherhood. For complicated reasons that belong in another book entirely, my marriage was also under enormous strain. And as I stood in the middle of this typhoon called my life, my little high-achiever self was all out of answers. So, at age thirty-five, I resigned from my law firm, sold my house, and moved my family to Tucson, Arizona, to start over.

Interestingly, as I explained this monumental decision to many bewildered friends and family, I framed it as "front-ending my retirement." In my mind, retirement was the prize at the end of this hellish slog called adulthood, and I was just going to take a little bit of my prize early. I figured I could borrow a decade of retirement at age thirty-five, reallocate my time to family and motherhood, and then make some more money later. *And so what if retirement happens at seventy instead of sixty?* I mused. This whole justification was hilariously thin. As if "retirement" held some intrinsic answer to my problems.

As you will read later in this book, after the initial euphoria wore off, I found myself inexplicably confused and deeply insecure. All of my indicia of success were gone or irrelevant. Not a single person I met in Tucson had ever heard of my illustrious law firm. No one cared about the billion-dollar deals I had closed. None of those skills made me a better mother or spouse. My ability to multitask and perform under pressure were woefully misplaced in the more laid-back city where I had chosen to live.

As I began to unpack all this during early-morning meetings with my French press and my journal, I could see that I had conflated who I was with what I had accomplished. I had merged the external proof of my success with my sense of self-worth. I had unthinkingly become a driven, intense, anxious "human doing" instead of a human being. Desperate enough to conclude that I must be missing something (maybe everything), I started to read books I never would have entertained before. Books about psychology, identity, spirituality, motivation. I explored a wide-ranging set of ideas and theories about what it means to thrive, as opposed to succeed. In this quest for understanding, I began to reconstruct my sense of who I was underneath all the outer roles I played in life: spouse, mother, lawyer, friend. I started to experiment with new ways to move through my days. I learned how to push myself out of my comfort zone professionally, tackling new (and terrifying) roles like business owner and writer.

Like so many of the wonderful disasters we navigate over time, the annihilation of my former life offered me the gift of discovering a new world of possibility. As I reshaped my identity and routines, I documented the questions and explorations that had been most helpful to me. And in that way, I laid the foundations of the Encore Program, which I have been facilitating in one way or another since 2009. As I guided more and more professionals who were at the edge of a career change like retirement (whether by choice or circumstance), I could see the same patterns and themes that defined my own challenge. At the time of this writing, fifteen years later, I have had the privilege of working with hundreds of high-achieving career professionals as they prepare to chart their course into a new chapter of life. This book is a collected offering of the insights, strategies, and tactics that help smooth the transition out of an intense career and prime the path forward with energizing and approachable possibility.

PART ONE

---∞∞⋘◆⋙∞∞---

RETIREMENT ANXIETY
When Liberation Feels Like Loss

chapter one

THE CONFUSING TABOO OF RETIREMENT

*If one does not know to which port one
is sailing, no wind is favorable.*

~ *Lucius Annaeus Seneca, Roman philosopher*

I was having lunch at a bar in Washington, DC, recently when a gentleman in a tailored suit came in and joined two younger men installed at nearby barstools. Both of them were gigantic, probably professional athletes. The guy in the suit had to be a sports lawyer, and he looked like he was in his mid-sixties.

"Hey, guys, so good to see you!" He shook their large hands and, after an exchange of niceties, sat down to talk business.

"Well, I really appreciate your getting together with me today because we have a few things to talk about," said the lawyer.

One of the giant men leaned forward and grinned, "When I talked with your secretary to set up this meeting, she told me not to mention the *R* word."

The lawyer started laughing. "Oh, I guess we're going to have to talk about that, aren't we?"

It hit me that the man in the suit was facing a very uncomfortable conversation about his impending retirement. The reluctance to even use the word says it all. Clearly, everyone was dancing around the great taboo of his retreat from the practice of law—what it meant for these athletes, who would next be advising them, and when the handover would take place. "I'm just going to step back a little," I later heard the lawyer demur. For all his efforts to underplay the moment, my guess was he was only stirring up more concern and confusion.

Even the etymology of the word *retire* drops a clue as to why people don't like it. In Middle French, *retirer* meant to withdraw or pull back. Modern definitions continue this theme of retreating, withdrawing, or receding. Unfortunately, the word gives us no indication of forward motion or expansion into something new, leaving those on this precipice in quite an existential quagmire.

Thanks to my fifteen years of guiding intense professionals as they plan for life after their careers, I am all too familiar with the squirming discomfort they often feel about the topic of their own retirement. In fact, the closer it gets, the more concerning it becomes. It is a bit like being marched toward an abyss that is somehow supposed to seem appealing. For some, the idea of change is welcome, but the absence of a plan is disturbing. For others, retirement equates with an appalling loss of who they are and what they love to do. This condition is made even worse by the celebratory attitude surrounding them—everyone else is ready to break out the champagne while the soon-to-be "retiree" is, at best, feeling unsettled and, at worst, feeling rather terrified. And then comes the relentless but confounding question: "What are you going to do?" All too often, my clients (who are accustomed to having answers) are utterly stumped.

I've Done Everything Right, So Why Do I Feel Lost?

The odyssey of work doesn't go on forever. Toward the end of even the most epic career, there comes a time when the hero must set sights on their inevitable landing. I have a stark memory of one of our early clients, Jim, who embodied this contradiction well. At the time, he was widely known and respected in his field as one of the greats. I felt privileged even to meet him, much less to guide him in his thinking about life after retirement. He was physically imposing, quietly powerful, humble in his bearing. When we asked him what brought him to us, he answered in a low voice. "Well, I feel like I'm running toward the edge of a cliff. I have no idea what I will do or who I will be in sixty days."

I was struck by the paradox before me. Here was a capable and accomplished leader who had excelled at the highest levels. In his own words, he was still at the top of his game. He was making the choice to retire because it was the right thing to do for his organization and for his younger colleagues, who were ready to step up to the opportunities his exit would create. His retirement was an intentional and selfless act. He had been a diligent saver and felt confident about his financial security. And yet, despite his volition, ability, and track records of success, here he sat before us without the first idea what the rest of his life would be about. "I'm terrified, if you want the truth," he said.

How can this be? For most, the idea of retiring has been a huge motivation for working hard and saving money. Many have deferred their dreams of extended travel, passion projects, or time with family for that distant point in the future when they will be done trading their freedom for income. And their families have been waiting for that same moment—when the hard-charging professional is finally free from their cell phone and can sink into the pleasure of simply being present with them.

But professionals become habituated to the constant stream of content, problem solving, and heroic levels of service to work demands. They are very good at what they do and often have the pleasure of reading about their work in the media. The idea of wandering around the house all day induces bolts of anxiety, yet there seems to be no obvious way to transfer their skills to another arena. To make matters worse, their own families have grave concerns about their well-being when the demands of working life are behind them. Will they lose their reason for living, or will they micromanage everyone around them? These are real concerns that arise from an upcoming retirement. And even if the idea of a less intense life is broadly appealing, the lack of a blueprint for that life is deeply worrisome.

Of course, all of them have done exactly what they were told to do to prepare for retirement. They have diligently saved a substantial percentage of their prodigious incomes every year. They usually have a conservative investment strategy guided by professional advisers. They've run every financial scenario to the ground and are told that they cannot realistically spend all the money they have. So they wonder, *What is this gnawing dread about? Why is the prospect of financial freedom combined with lots of free time so daunting? And who can I talk to about this quandary?*

To make matters worse, most professionals in this common predicament feel oddly isolated. Few speak openly about retirement, and many wait until the last possible moment to tell colleagues and clients it is happening. Retirement is almost like a shameful secret in their world, to be avoided at all costs, despite the increasing pressure across professional services industries to retire earlier than ever. On top of feeling lost, the retiring professional feels alone, often wondering if they are the only person who can't figure this thing out. On that score, they could not be more wrong.

Almost as Stressful as Jailtime

Jim isn't alone in finding the concept of retirement stressful. His is a normal and natural reaction to the fear of losing one's professional identity, primary life structure, relevance in the world, main purpose, the sense of making a difference, and overall source of validation. The negative outcomes associated with this anxiety are dismaying.

As one historical example, in 1967, psychiatrists Thomas Holmes and Richard Rahe looked at the links between stress

6

and illness (such as heart attacks, strokes, and cancer) associated with forty-three significant life events ranging from the death of a spouse to being charged with a minor traffic infraction. After analyzing the medical records of over five thousand patients, Holmes and Rahe confirmed a statistically valid link between these taxing life events and impending illness. They ranked events as more or less stressful based on the likelihood of having a "health breakdown" within two years. The scale they came up with, best known as the Holmes-Rahe Life Stress Inventory, ranked retirement as the tenth most potent stressor out of the forty-three studied, assigning it a stress score of forty-five points out of a total possible one hundred.[1] Retiring from a career, the scale showed, is only slightly less stressful than being diagnosed with a serious illness or being thrown behind bars! No wonder Jim was feeling unsettled, and no wonder not everyone is ready to uncork the bubbly when this moment is finally upon them.

Holmes and Rahe Stress Scale

#	LIFE EVENT (STRESSOR)	VALUE
1	Death of spouse/child	100
2	Divorce	73
3	Marital separation	65
4	Jail term	63
5	Death of close family member	63
6	Major personal injury or illness	63
7	Marriage	60
8	Fired from work	47
9	Marital reconciliation	45
10	Retirement	45
11	Major change in health of family member	44

---

[1]   T. H. Holmes and R. H. Rahe, "The Social Readjustment Rating Scale," *Journal of Psychosomatic Research* 11 no. 2 (1967): 213–218.

The perceived stress associated with retirement is easy to understand. Along with the end of a career come the threatened losses of identity, community, structure, and purpose—and money alone does not neatly solve any of those losses. It naturally follows that if one is not feeling empowered to move through these modifications in an intentional and confident way, one is at risk for a negative outcome. When we share the Holmes-Rahe findings, we often hear our clients breathe a sigh of relief. There's hard data behind the anxieties they're experiencing. *Oh, this is a normal thing—it isn't just my ineptitude*, they realize.

More recent studies, including those conducted on populations outside the US, continue to support the Holmes-Rahe findings. A May 2013 discussion paper published by the UK's Institute of Economic Affairs presented research showing that retirement increases the chances of suffering from clinical depression by around 40 percent and of having at least one diagnosed physical illness by 60 percent.[2] If you know you're anxious about the idea of retiring and march yourself into it anyway, there's a real risk you will experience some or all of the symptoms associated with that dangerous route. Unaddressed feelings of retirement anxiety can lead to:

- Loss of energy
- Isolation
- Reduced self-esteem
- Stagnation
- Lack of confidence
- Depression
- Strained personal relationships
- Increased dependence on substances
- Increased risk for illness or early morbidity

---

[2] Gabriel H. Sahlgren, "Work Longer, Live Healthier," Institute of Economic Affairs, Discussion Paper No. 46, May 2013.

These stress symptoms can coalesce into a downward spiral, and the deeper that spiral, the harder it is to turn around.

The work we do, while exploring possibility and opportunity in a person's next chapter of life, is equally about ensuring that each individual can successfully manage themselves through the change of retirement in a way that supports psychological health and dodges pitfalls like depression, contraction, and illness. We are not selling a Pollyanna story that everything is always going to be glorious in retirement. The disruption and loss inherent in any major life transition are potentially fraught with emotional triggers. This is why we take a proactive approach by helping people map a path to their greatest possibility of happiness and new opportunity. For high-performing humans, whose identities are inextricably linked to their professional accomplishments, we help turn retirement anxiety into genuine excitement about what's possible in the future.

Bottom line: retirement anxiety is a real thing, and the topic of retirement can feel truly threatening for people who have invested so much in their professional identity. It is not all fun and games or cruises and golf. Not only can retirement anxiety pose a real risk to a retiring person's physical and mental health but it can also have negative impacts on their clients, colleagues, and firm or company.

A successful lawyer we advised comes to mind as an example of this phenomenon. Steve, so used to mastery, competence, and control, was quietly and desperately dealing with retirement anxiety. The almost robotic tone of his voice gave him away the day we met him, and he had previously selected several target dates for his dreaded departure, only to push them back again and again as they approached. He felt deeply uncomfortable committing to or discussing his retirement, and now that his firm was pressuring him to go, his passive resistance was flaring into overt anger. The idea of being put out to pasture was very upsetting to Steve. He's not the kind of guy who's used to being shown the door.

Steve found himself working harder than ever, still focused on billable hours and revenue generation, even as the metrics began to lose economic meaning for him. On top of all this, his repeated efforts to generate plans for postcareer engagement had yielded a single idea: learn bridge. With no sense of how to move forward, Steve understandably found himself clinging to his known world for dear life, creating problems not just for himself but also for his firm, younger colleagues, and clients.

And this highlights another negative of retirement anxiety: the lack of proactive succession planning. Steve was still bringing in clients as if he would remain the primary lawyer on their matters. He was not transferring his client relationships to younger partners to ensure that his clients and his prestigious practice—and even his legacy, for that matter—would remain intact after his exit. Apart from the toll this was taking on Steve personally, there were negative implications for his firm, clients, and colleagues. If the formula for success for a lawyer like Steve is to build deep and enduring relationships with institutional clients, then the failure to engage in proactive succession planning is like losing a well-played game in the fourth quarter. I will discuss effective approaches to succession planning in detail later in this book. For now, suffice it to recognize that retirement anxiety can have very tangible costs beyond the well-being of the person who is retiring. Get it right and there are positive, enduring benefits for the firm; get it wrong, and the negative consequences for both teams and clients can be significant.

Haunted by Negative Examples

Almost everyone has at least one example of a colleague or family member who retired without a plan for engagement and experienced severe decline. Though the particulars may differ, the broad stories recur with startling predictability. We hear over and over about people who avoided the preparations, assumed they would figure it out eventually, and then slowly faded over a period of months, finding it harder and harder to energize new endeavors. The protagonists of these stories invariably meet with sad endings. Instead of gliding into a contented retirement, they fall into the wreckage of a collapsing life. The differences between improvision and well-laid design are at play in the sagas of retirees who chose the former and suffered mightily.

As much as a positive role model can inspire empowered action, a negative one can imply certain doom. We observed this phenomenon when one of our clients, a prominent tech executive, lamented, "I don't have any role models for retiring well." John had reason to be discouraged. We soon learned why as he relayed the tragedy of his well-regarded mentor, Rick, who had taught John much of what he ultimately parlayed into a successful career. California wine country had always held great appeal for Rick. As his retirement approached, he snapped up fifty acres along the central coast and built an imposing mansion for himself and his wife. Replete with commanding views of rolling farmland and easy gateways to vintners, it was far removed from the hustle and bustle of San Francisco yet close to his idyll. There wasn't a soul in sight to disturb their bucolic peace. The externalities couldn't have been better, and many assumed that Rick had created the perfect life in retirement. How it felt on the inside gave way to a different reality.

As John recounted, "It was just a disaster. I would go out and visit him, and he and his wife were intoxicated every day by lunchtime." Rick ultimately drank himself to an early death. With this dire and dystopic plunge as John's most accessible example of retirement, it was no wonder he had concerns for himself.

Allow me to reconstruct two legacies of retirement, both taken from my family history, that informed my own thinking about retirement. I'm talking about my father and maternal grandfather, and the contrast between them couldn't be starker. Grandpa was a general in the United States Air Force, but at age ninety, he was busy planting an apple orchard that would take ten years to bear fruit. He lived to be ninety-three, so he never saw those trees bloom. Yet he remained engaged and vibrant up until the day he died. My grandfather treated life like it would continue forever. He was an example of someone who never failed to have numerous projects ongoing at any time.

My father enacted the antithesis. He was the sort of person who needed to stay within a familiar framework and be of service to others. When he retired, he was the head of the facilities department of a local university. He finally set down that position in his early seventies. Over the next six years, Dad descended into severe alcoholism, physical decline, and isolation. He just withdrew little by little. It was like watching him die slowly.

My dad was born in 1936. For him and many men of his generation, retirement represented a free pass to harboring no obligations. What he failed to appreciate was that having people need him and rely on him gave his life very deep meaning. When he let that go, he lost his purpose. He didn't find value in just lounging around. So he ended up engaging in what felt like the freedom to drink in the middle of the day.

At first, that may have felt liberating and fun. But it became an insidious lead indictor of ultimate decline. The ticking time bomb on that descent started the first day of his retirement. He was like a different person after he left his working life.

The opposing stories of my father and my grandfather grounded my personal perspective on retirement. Their different approaches highlighted for me how thin the "retirement dream" really is. The notion that having enough money in the bank somehow equates to a formula for a satisfying life is tragically flawed. It's simply not the case for most people, and sometimes what seem like obvious choices in retirement can, without an intentional strategy, lead to surprisingly bad outcomes.

For example, many people, much like Rick, imagine relocating as part of their retirement solution, whether to mitigate tax burdens, experience milder climates, or embrace a more bucolic lifestyle. These are all terrific reasons to consider a new home base, but without a game plan to fertilize a new community, there is a risk of isolation and loneliness. It's not the first thing people think about when they dream about pulling up stakes. Instead, they fancy, *Oh, we'll no longer be stuck in traffic! The air will be pure and fresh! We'll see golden sunsets every evening!* It sounds amazing—and it can be. But think about the relationships, providers, and activities being left behind and the possibility of social isolation in a new context.

Social isolation can literally be a killer. It's associated with markedly increased rates of cognitive decline, heart disease, stroke, depression, and suicide among older adults. People need people, as we all learned from the 2020 pandemic.

None of this is to say relocating will never work out. As I'll explore more deeply later in this book, New Yorkers-turned-Wyomingites Margaret "Peggy" Andrews Davenport and her husband, Kirk Davenport, are living proof that a move can go smashingly well. It's always going to be an adjustment. But the first steps are developing an understanding of what the new place offers in terms of growth opportunities and community and how to deploy oneself authentically.

Peggy and Kirk decided to retire together at the peak of their rock star careers. She was fifty-five years old and a pivotal partner at a top law firm, where she first co-chaired its private equity group and later its corporate department. He was fifty-seven and an alpha member of the New York–based corporate department of another top law firm. Both were positioned in the top tier of Chambers and Partners, one of the world's leading legal ranking companies.

The power couple came to us in 2016 wanting to make the most of their next chapter. With their combined assets, the prospect of generating additional income was no longer a pressing priority. They were free to follow their hearts. Kirk and Peggy had been going to Jackson Hole, Wyoming, for many years. Kirk had parceled his energy into designing a beautiful home where the couple would live and entertain. Much thoughtful and detailed planning went into his concept. It wasn't just, "Hey, let's move!" because, as seductive as it may be, moving is never simple. The open question for both spouses was *How are we going to be useful and engaged in our new community? We are not people who can subsist on leisure alone.* I will share much more of their story later in this book.

The bottom line is that meaning, engagement, and community continue to matter after an intense career. As my husband and cofacilitator, David, once said while presenting to a group of senior law firm partners, "In our experience, no one in this cohort wants 365 Saturdays in a row." It got a laugh from the crowd then, and it always gets a bemused "Absolutely!" now. Another adage that resonates with our audience comes from basketballer Abe Lemons: "The trouble with retirement is that you never get a day off." In our experience, these truisms resonate because we've all seen people who seem to be riding into the sunset but go right over the edge—and that's just scary.

Endings Matter

While much of dealing with retirement is about what comes next, it is equally vital to consider the psychological and emotional importance of the ending itself. When a significant career comes to a conclusion, there are inevitable losses, which brings us to a little-discussed part of retiring: grieving those losses.

Grief can include a complex of emotions such as sadness, despair, confusion, and even anger. What's the anger about? Some psychologists argue that the feeling of empowerment that anger unleashes masks the more painful sense of vulnerability, thereby energizing a capacity for action. Seen in this light, anger is an instinctive and adaptive response to threat. When we experience a significant loss, especially one we do not choose or control, we often chafe under a sense of injustice that something we treasure has been taken away from us. This sort of loss can manifest in angry feelings like resentment, frustration, or even rage, as we struggle to come to terms with the unfairness of the situation.

A client of ours shared a poignant story about one of his former colleagues, Matthew, who was slowly pressured to retire from his firm after forty years as an import-export lawyer. The firm's strategy had shifted over time, and far from investing resources in continuing his practice, the firm had been hinting for years that it might be time for him to go. Eventually, it started cutting his compensation and refusing to hire junior help. Finally, Matthew was told he could either retire or be terminated. Five years later, our client reported, Matthew still thinks of himself as an out-of-work import-export lawyer and is deeply embittered toward the law firm in which he invested so many years of his life. Unprocessed grief and anger are, sadly, the defining features of Matthew's retirement.

We see grieving as a natural and necessary part of processing a significant ending like retirement and oft-associated loss of identity. For one, grieving helps acknowledge the reality of the loss in the first place. Denial or avoidance of a loss can lead to a prolonged state of confusion, disbelief, and distress. It is important to recognize that many positive aspects of a decades-long career are going away, be it a successful work identity, a nexus of social interactions, or the mental stimuli and routine that organized the day. The more a person feels they have been stripped of these survival tools unfairly, the more likely the eruptions of ire and indignation.

And while grieving is almost always a helpful part of our clients' retirement experience, emotion is typically hard for our clients to express, especially in a professional context. To get a seasoned professional or executive to admit sadness to his or her colleagues would be a monumental task. But we remind them that the ability to engage proactively with feelings, even negative ones, is a powerful skill.

Jim Dethmer of the Conscious Leadership Group, in his work coaching leaders and high performers, expounds on how emotional intelligence surpasses IQ in the workplace. He demystifies the topic of feelings and emotion, explaining that emotions are just energy in motion in the body. Emotion always creates a physical sensation. Dethmer posits that our emotions exist as a potent signaling device and are designed to get our attention but then need to be processed or released. But because many of us are taught throughout our lives to repress emotion, this unreleased energy can end up literally stuck in our craw. At worst, unprocessed emotion can make us sick, but it almost always leads to chronic rumination, as with Matthew, recycling the same negative feelings until they harden into long-term bitterness.

Further, a negative ending can have an outsize bearing on how an entire experience is remembered. Divorce exemplifies this phenomenon. For some, when they recall a prior marriage, the final few years, followed by a painful split, made the entire relationship seem horrendous, even if a substantial part of it was quite happy. A body of psychology helps explain why. The rule in this matter says that an experience is evaluated and recalled from its most intense point, from its end point, or both. How we remember events is strongly influenced by our lens on peak events we've experienced instead of the sum total of the experience. Nobel Prize–winner Daniel Kahneman minted the so-called peak-end theory, and other psychologists including Chip and Dan Heath further explored this bias in how we form memories. In the Heaths' book *The Power of Moments: Why Certain Experiences Have Extraordinary Impact*, they wrote:

> When people assess an experience, they tend to forget or ignore its length—a phenomenon called "duration neglect." Instead, they seem to rate the experience based on two key moments: (1) the best or worst moment, known as the "peak"; and (2) the ending. . . . What's indisputable is that when we assess our experiences, we don't average our minute-by-minute sensations. Rather, we tend to remember flagship moments: the peaks, the pits, and the transitions.[3]

---

[3] Chip Heath and Dan Heath, *The Power of Moments: Why Certain Experiences Have Extraordinary Impact* (New York, NY: Simon & Schuster, 2017).

The relevance for retirement is obvious. One could have had thirty-eight vibrant years in their career. But if they leave on a sour note, it can color recollections about the entire experience. Creating a positive and empowered transition into retirement helps mitigate the risk that an unhappy ending translates into the sense of having had an unhappy career—a dreadful result for people who have often loved and given much to their working lives.

Chapter Summary

Retirement anxiety is common among intense professionals, resulting in an avoidance of the topic altogether.

Although many professionals considering retirement feel alone in their anxiety, research supports the proposition that retirement is a stressful experience for most people.

Research validates that the stressors associated with retiring are significant enough that they can cause or contribute to a negative health event.

Unaddressed anxiety about retirement can lead to numerous conscious and unconscious behaviors, including trouble in letting go of responsibilities and clients—the opposite of proactive and intentional succession planning.

Retirement anxiety is fueled by negative examples of people with money, time, and freedom who enter into rapid decline and early death.

There is a measure of grieving that accompanies the end of a meaningful career. Recognizing and allowing for that grief is part of ending a career in a positive way, especially because the way things end often colors how we later perceive the entire experience.

chapter two

THE PROBLEM WITH THE RETIREMENT CONSTRUCT

A life oriented to pure leisure is, in the end, a life oriented to death—the greatest leisure of all.

~ *Ann Lamott, author, quoting her father, Kenneth Lamott*

Retirement's Origin Story

How did we get here? Where did the concept of retirement come from? Perhaps you know someone who's grappling with retirement, or you are on the verge of it—or perhaps you just moved through this experience yourself. Many feel sheepish because they don't have it all figured out. *How is it that I was looking forward to this twenty years ago? I saved all my money, and now that it's two years away, I'm dreading it. What the heck am I missing here?*

It's a funny thing about retirement. We all talk about work's end as if it's a place we go, an outcome we eventually live, or an identity we have to embrace: I am a "retiree." I have retired. I am doing [fill in the blank] in retirement. The phenomenon is an artifact of our culture. Yet it is also a myth. Retirement is not a place, an outcome, or an identity. It's an inflection point, like college graduation or any other accomplishment, when completion flows naturally into new opportunity. No one walks around saying "I'm a graduate" for the rest of their life because it's plainly just one threshold among the many they will go on to cross. They move through the moment, they high-five, and they get on to the next thing. So how did retirement become so laden? When did this cultural artifact take shape?

The original idea of retirement bubbled up from the political ground of late nineteenth-century Prussia. In 1881, Otto von Bismarck, the conservative minister president of Prussia, maneuvered to woo unemployed youth away from the burgeoning socialist movement. The scheme he devised would pay senior citizens to leave the workforce. "Those who are disabled from work by age and invalidity have a well-grounded claim to care from the state"; his words resounded in the Reichstag. Bismarck's old-age pension program entered into law in 1889, making Prussia (now Germany) the first nation to support retirement. At a time when the ethos was "Work until you die," punching the clock for the last time at sixty-five or even seventy constituted a radical idea.

The idea started to spread across Europe, and by the 1920s, it had reached the United States. Banking, oil, and railroad sectors began offering pensions to their employees: If you stay with us until a certain age, we'll take care of you when you leave us. In the US, the Social Security Act of 1935 crystallized this notion into a social insurance program to give retired workers aged sixty-five or older a continuing income. Yet for all its ostensible enlightenment, the provision cast a dubious glow. Was setting the age for benefits at sixty-five—when the average life expectancy for a working American man was fifty-eight—really designed to help people?

Whatever its intent, the new law trumpeted the hunch that at sixty-five, maybe you're meant to stop working, especially if you've already lived longer than most of your peers. However, over the rest of the twentieth century, America would see the greatest gains in life expectancy ever known, complicating this picture even further.

During this evolving story in the US came the Revenue Act of 1978 and its Internal Revenue Code Section 401(k), granting employees a tax-free way to defer compensation. That fateful section fueled what we now call the financial planning industry. Its boosters advertised hard: Let us manage your money so you can get your sailboat in your golden retirement. As we will see, the disappearance of senior citizens from the labor force holds no inherent logic. Rather, it's the consequence of a marketing story. Retirement has become so ingrained in how we think about working life that we don't even question it. It is almost like a rite of passage, only without any actual substance.

The Golden Years: Selling the Dream

The term *golden years* denotes the twilight of a lifespan spent in leisure. We all know the term. But how many of us realize it was coined for a retirement community ad campaign? The myth's animating spirit was first sloganized for the Sun City brand of retirement communities developed and launched in the Arizona desert by Del Webb in 1960. As reporter Steve Lohr described in a 2005 *New York Times* article, retirement got entangled with commercial representations of seniors basking in an idyllic, romanticized bubble. Yes, that's right. A real estate marketing campaign essentially defined the big dream of retiring into some blissful fantasyland. Retirees could move to these developments and luxuriate in the promise of "An Active, New Way of Life" for people "55 and better," per the Sun City brochure.

The Del E. Webb Construction Company's pitch helps explain how people in my father's generation formed ideas of how to retire. It was not an approach premised in scientific research into well-being later in life. It was designed to sell real estate. It was a powerful sales pitch. As Lohr observed, conditions in the fifties enabled it to take root in American soil.

[I]t was the post-World War II ascent of the American economy that truly laid the groundwork for mass retirement. Executives and union leaders recognized the longer lives and greater affluence of many workers, but what was still missing, they said, was an alluring model of life after work.[4]

We're all walking around with some of these threads of "the new leisure set" marketing story. So it's understandable that we don't think about planning comprehensively. But this also explains why it's so dangerous to limit our thinking to a financial analysis of how to afford idle comforts. If the real estate sector originated the "friendly years" narrative, over time, other industries contributed to the reductive way we think about retirement.

Sporting a sensible blue blazer, actor Tommy Lee Jones stands in a bustling shopping mall and reports, "Ameriprise asked people a simple question: Can you keep your lifestyle in retirement?" Several passersby express their doubts before Tommy Lee plugs Ameriprise's exclusive "Confident Retirement Approach." Or watch "Larry," the eponymous retirement-planning geek, transfer funds from his Bank of America savings account into his retirement account at corporate sibling Merrill Edge. To the tune of Billy Joel's "My Life," we've seen Larry's younger self quit "his friend's leaf-raking business for not offering a 401(k)." Larry has always thought ahead.

Both TV commercials imply that financial resources translate into contentment. It's the message of countless commercials like them, often with seniors teeing off on the golf course or with silver-haired couples strolling blithely along a glistening shore. We've been marketed to in a somewhat unhelpful way when it comes to retirement. No doubt we all need to save for our later years, but the

---

[4]   Lohr, Steve. "The Late, Great 'Golden Years.'" *The New York Times*, March 6, 2005. https://www.nytimes.com/2005/03/06/weekinreview/the-late-great-golden-years.html?searchResultPosition=1.

subtext of these marketing narratives tells us that the life of pure leisure is all we want or need. As long as we get to idle away every day and have fun, that is enough. In theory, this may sound great when you're working full time. But the reality is well borne out: relaxation alone will not do.

The truth is that an abundance of financial resources is only as useful as the underlying purposes those resources serve. Money sitting in the bank means very little absent a practical application. It only acquires meaning when you liquidate it into a gift, an experience, or an opportunity to advance some aspect of your life that matters to you.

Here's where the disconnect with most of the marketing that clouds today's media environment comes in. Because the ads are all about reaching that moment of financial nirvana—implying that everything is handled and done with the release from material worries—they leave a void in our thinking about what we actually saved the money for. That's the real question that bears contemplation. It is within this search for meaning that opportunities for self-realization are revealed.

From the bible to *The Great Gatsby*, we know that abundance in and of itself is meaningless. The paradox of being liberated by abundance is that financial fulfillment cannot deliver the transcendent meaning associated with life satisfaction. If we accept the insidious message that we're just supposed to luxuriate carefree for the rest of our days, we're in for a rude awakening when it comes time to put this thin plan into action.

Still, the hype persists. It's easy to see why. Most of the ads are sponsored by insurance companies, banks, and mutual funds and targeted to mid-thirtysomethings in the thick of their working lives. Advertising works on the subconscious minds of consumers, persuading them to believe in its product claims, influencing their attitudes, and ultimately changing their behavior. That's the point of marketing: to shape our subconscious choices. The money managers are selling a dream of what it's going to be like when all our efforts to produce wealth are finally behind us. But the dream is not so great when you're standing at the edge of it.

My clients are invariably troubled by the mythical "retirement story" that has grown out of this history. This story led them to sacrifice, sweat, and save for several decades to arrive at a moment in time when, adequate money in the bank, they get to stop working and do whatever they want to do. And herein lies the rub because the obvious choices seem unappealing. If they are on the younger end of the spectrum, they will live on permanent vacation for the rest of their lives (sailboats, golf, exotic travel, and such). Or if they are older, this is probably the beginning of the end, but at least they can die peacefully with lots of money in the bank. As attributed to Kenneth Lamott by his daughter Ann in *Bird by Bird*, "A life oriented to pure leisure is, in the end, a life oriented to death—the greatest leisure of all." No thanks.

If you're reading this book at all, I suspect you do not care to embrace either of these paths—pure leisure or decline leading to death. Yet our cultural associations with retirement, along with our limited approach to planning, leave us with little else to imagine. As I noted earlier, even the word *retirement* is problematic, with its modern meaning of "withdrawal from one's position or occupation or from active working life." I can assure you that our clients cannot envision a satisfying world where the primary verb is "withdraw," and life is defined by the absence of an "active working life."

Instead of Retirement, Think Graduation

The act of retirement doesn't have to lead us inexorably down one of those paths. Retirement can be a turning point brimming with opportunity, a moment of life leading to new direction and challenge, a time when our best years remain ahead. But to have a fulfilling postcareer life, we need to do some planning beyond our financial realm and look for inspiration aside from beaches, golf courses, and sailboats.

When we first sit down with our clients, we ask them how they feel about the notion of retiring. The common themes are stark. We hear things like, "I absolutely hate that word—let's not use it." Or "I'm really not sure—I know I feel very unsettled by the idea, but even worse—I have no framework for how to approach it." Or "I haven't said this to anybody, but the truth is, I'm terrified because I have no idea what's about to happen to my life."

At this juncture, we encourage a reframe of the looming inflection point from one of contraction (implied by the word *retirement*) to one of expansion, like one might feel at a graduation. Almost instantly, we see a shift in our clients' energy at this suggestion. Now the focus is on what else is possible, having already achieved so much, instead of what is being left behind. Often, a new anxiety emerges because the possibilities can seem both endless and daunting, stoking a different type of perplexity.

Of course, we assure them they are in very good company. Our clients almost always share a sense of overwhelm and uncertainty at the start of our work together and imagine that they are alone in their confusion. We quickly assure them, for the reasons I have already detailed, that many people, especially those leaving intense careers, are similarly flummoxed.

The Paradox of Choice

Imagine it's a hot summer day, and you pass by a gelato shop brimming with scrumptious flavors. Which would be better, tiramisu, cioccolato, or the sundry other temptations? Winnowing such a selection down to a favorite can jam your ability to choose. Whether determining something as consequential as your options after retirement or just picking an ice cream to suit your mood, you might experience indecision when faced with multiple options that you struggle to compare.

Decision paralysis is a topic we discuss with every client. As we point out, the very conditions that make this moment feel daunting also constitute the raw materials for the most opportune moment they may ever have lived. For the first time, they have financial security, an abundance of time, deep experience and knowledge, a pervasive network, and an understanding of how the world works. The paradox is that the very conditions that translate into a surge of options and opportunities can also block the ability to decide out of fear of making the wrong choice.

A common stress signal we'll hear includes feeling rushed to determine their postwork future or bouncing around cluelessly without the comfort of side walls. Our job is to reorient a client's thinking. Whatever the exact wording we use, it will invariably convey the following idea: you have as many skills and assets as you have ever had, and now the challenge is to combine them in a way that feels energizing and expansive. We then follow up with some reassurance along these lines: where you're standing, it feels like a problem, but it's actually a huge opportunity. To clinch the redirect, we acknowledge that they're no longer floundering in a vacuum but, rather, are launched on a results-oriented path toward a desirable outcome. Without a plan to organize your retirement, it feels like an impossible puzzle to put together. We're here to help you build a road map to new purpose and meaning.

Finding New Role Models

It takes some digging, but there are plenty of people who find a new gear in late adulthood, after their "career" has come to an end. Peter Drucker is one such example. I first heard Drucker's story when business management guru Jim Collins appeared on a podcast called *The Tim Ferriss Show* in 2019. Peter Drucker was a very prolific thinker and writer in the area of business and management and was one of the first people to think deeply about knowledge workers. He traced the transition from the industrial revolution, when people toiled with their hands, to the technology revolution of the twentieth century that swelled the ranks of those working with their minds. Among the issues that intrigued him was "How do we manage people who are knowledge workers and not manual laborers?"

Collins recounted his formative meeting with the Vienna-born father of management thinking when Collins was in his mid-thirties and Drucker in his mid-eighties. By age sixty-five, Drucker had only published fourteen of his thirty-nine books. He lived to be ninety-five, and after Collins sat down with him, the elder sage would go on to write and publish ten more books. I love Drucker's story: at sixty-five, he was just getting started, and at eighty-five, he was far from done.

Although marketing narratives have given us plenty of empty examples of what the last quarter of life might look like, here are four more examples of individuals who had noteworthy achievements in late adulthood. Julia Child got her career cooking at age forty-nine. That's when the late bloomer wrote her first cookbook. At fifty-one, she pioneered the concept of a television cooking show with her PBS hit *The French Chef.* She would take home three Emmys and a Peabody, author numerous books, win the French Legion of Honor, and broadcast hundreds of kitchen episodes over the very busy next decades of her life. Gladys Burrill had climbed mountains, trekked across deserts, ridden horses, and become a multi-engine airplane pilot before running her first marathon at age eighty-six. By ninety-two, she was named the oldest female marathon runner by *The Guinness Book of World Records.*

Laurel Ritchie has a great story too. She made history as the first African American to lead a major sports league when she became president of the Women's National Basketball Association just shy of the big five-o. Her varied pursuits after five seasons at the WNBA helm included chairing the board of Dartmouth College. Dr. Hubert Jones is another senior legend. By his late sixties, "Hubie" had clocked sixteen years as a dean at Boston University—like Ritchie, he was the first African American in the role. So it wasn't like he needed a new gig when he founded the Boston Children's Chorus upon hitting his seventies. Yet the music-themed vehicle for social healing and community building took off. As an encore, he began Higher Ground, a program inspired by the Harlem Children's Zone to empower youth and their families with social, educational, and community-building services. Jones has clocked six decades and counting as a social worker, academic, community organizer, and civic leader, and he shows no signs of letting up.

I share these stories as a reminder that our opportunities remain abundant and interesting in our later decades, when we are arguably positioned more favorably than at any point in our past. As we contemplate life after an intense career, we are equipped with financial security, the wisdom of experience, a terrific network, a true understanding of what we are capable of—and, at last, an open canvas of time to create whatever masterpiece we can imagine.

Chapter Summary

Retirement originated as a political tool, not a well-being tool.

Retirement marketing has created a lot of mythology, leading to two extremes in many people's minds: either imminent decline or permanent vacation.

When reframed, "retirement" presents an incredible opportunity, a graduation into more rather than a slide into less.

Ironically, many people find the number of new directions available to them overwhelming and need a framework to sort and evaluate them.

There are plenty of inspiring examples of people who found new levels of meaning, contribution, and satisfaction after their primary careers, and these role models can help light the way.

chapter three

CHANGE: FROM APPREHENSION TO ENTHUSIASM

A ship is safe in the harbor—but that's
not what ships are built for.

~ John Shedd, businessman, civic
leader, and philanthropist

So, What Do You Do?

Allow me to take you back to a rather embarrassing moment in mid-2004. I am in Tucson, Arizona, where I have recently moved with my first husband and two small children, ages one and three. Six months earlier, I had "retired" from a very intense career with a Wall Street law firm at age thirty-five because I could not make the eighty-hour workweek fit with motherhood. I am standing in a room trying to meet new people at a women's networking event. I have just told someone for the fifth time, when asked what I do, that "I used to be a lawyer with Milbank." Blank stare—again.

As I was driving home from that mortifying experience, it struck me that I had completely lost my sense of identity. I was clutching at my past to explain who I was, even to myself, which felt both safe and more than a little sad. Somehow, my concept of "front-ending" my retirement to focus on motherhood had left me rather rudderless. I imagined, of course, that I would alternately be stretched out on a yoga mat and finger painting with my kids, with some wine and entrepreneurship mixed in. That is not quite how it played out.

Now, let me be clear. For the first three months, I was pinching myself to make sure I had not died and gone to heaven. No more Blackberry buzzing constantly. (Remember—it was 2003.) No steady stream of incoming emails. No unexpected trips to New York City or three a.m. conference calls with people in Singapore who were planning to head to happy hour when we hung up. I was burned out, and as I caught up on my sleep, I thought I'd figure the rest out soon enough.

But after six months, I was filled with apprehensive thoughts. *Why am I feeling so restless? Why do I swing wildly between the stress of being late to preschool with the kids and then bored out of my head? Why have I alphabetized my spice cabinet? Why was I introducing myself by telling people who I used to be?* But if I was no longer the ass-kicking lawyer at the prestigious law firm, then who the hell was I? And why did this change I had chosen for myself feel so daunting?

As I like to say now, I handled that life change with the sure touch of the inexperienced. It was only several years later, after a great deal of reflection, research, and soul searching, that I understood how my sense of competence and mastery in my comfort zone had led me to mistakenly believe that no matter how aggressively and suddenly I changed my life, I would quickly land on my feet.

After the initial euphoria of my adrenaline-soaked move had worn off, I found myself inexplicably paralyzed by the twin losses of my identity as a successful professional and my highly structured and pressure-filled lifestyle. To say nothing of the loss of my community of friends and colleagues, my world of social activities, my beloved local haunts, and the never-ending intellectual stimulation.

All that richness just disappeared overnight. I went through then *exactly* what many of our clients are going through right now.

I was very confused about it all. I had always been able to brute-force my way forward. Paralysis was not a sensation I recognized. I found myself overwhelmed by the simplest tasks that should have been a breeze, but I had been used to having the firm organize so much for me. Silly stuff, like going to the post office, setting up my computer, making travel plans, buying office supplies. These things used to happen magically without my having to think about what went into making them happen. I also found that, despite my new-found "free time," I was still struggling to get to appointments on time and make it to the library before it closed. For the first time in my life, I found myself disorganized. Without the pressure of time scarcity that had driven me, I lost my operating system—a lifestyle of racing against an unrelenting series of impossible demands that put me at MACH 10 all the time. My mistaken assumption was that if I removed that pressure, I'd just relax straight into this newfound open space and calmly go about my day. Well, it wasn't that simple.

On top of that, I understood my professional skills in such a specific way that I could not begin to imagine how or where I could ever apply them in Tucson, Arizona. No one in this town needs a lawyer who can close a billion-dollar telecom deal. That left me feeling a bit like a thoroughbred racehorse that had been running on a specific track for a very long time and was now being put out to wander around the pasture. I had a precise and well-honed skill but nowhere to exercise it. My competence and mastery now felt like my greatest vulnerability.

To make matters worse, I found myself trying to kill the abundant time I could not otherwise seem to put to good use. Before my move, I had never watched even one episode of *Oprah*. Daytime TV was not a feature of my life. But now I found myself drifting onto the sofa just to numb the constant anxiety. I felt beside myself, which so nicely captures the fact that I was no longer in sync with *me*. While I was enormously grateful for my expanded experience of motherhood, the rest of my Venn diagram was woefully empty.

Restless, anxious, I wasn't enjoying the peace and stillness and expansive space to think. None of that was pleasing to me. Far from reveling in the endless worlds that now opened up, I felt stuck in a simulacrum of repose. Looking back, I had made too many changes too abruptly. But at the time, I could not even begin to name the problem, much less solve it. The longer this went on, the more embarrassed and lost I felt. And the harder it became to create forward momentum. Eventually, I discovered something called the comfort zone. It all started to make sense. It turns out that leaving an intense career with no game plan can be completely destabilizing. Understanding the psychology of the comfort zone and how the brain responds to change helps explain why this is so.

The Paradox of the Comfort Zone

While your comfort zone is, to state the obvious, comfortable, it can contribute to some surprising downsides when facing a major change like retirement. For starters, a long stretch in your comfort zone naturally makes you feel masterful. But if that very sense of mastery leads you to thoughtlessly, even arrogantly, leap into too much change too suddenly, the resulting stress dump may overwhelm your brain's capacity to smoothly change and adapt. How do you feel about your ability to control your situation now? Probably not so good. The three-pound organ that defines your humanity can short-circuit when overloaded. At this point, the hundred billion firing neurons that wire together to process your thoughts, emotions, and behaviors become stuck in a loop of cumulative negative stress. The persistent pressure this exerts on your brain circuits isn't a character flaw. Rather, it's the interplay of biology with your experience. That state of feeling frozen in a no-exit zone can make it very difficult to think your way out of confusion, build new relationships, or even be productive.

Second, too much time in our comfort zones can actually lead to reduced learning, growth, and performance, as several studies have demonstrated. Any of us can relate to the feeling of boredom and stagnation that can ensue. Brain science tells us that our incentives for learning plateau if we lollygag within the cushy confines of safety from risk. How this cozy behavioral state relates to the inflection point of retirement introduces a splash of behavioral psychology into the conversation with our clients, and it is worth reviewing here.

Though Judith M. Bardwick coined the term *comfort zone* in her 1991 book *Danger in the Comfort Zone*, psychologists Robert Yerkes and John Dodson pioneered an experiment showing the connection between arousal and performance as far back as 1908. They observed that mice ran to the end of their mazes more readily when administered electric shocks of incremental intensity—up to a certain threshold. Too many jolts sent them seeking cover instead of soldiering on. The resulting Yerkes-Dodson law holds for humans as well. Arousal or stress can be a motivating factor, but only after and up to a point. When stress levels become too low or too high, our performance flags.

The research duo used the term *optimal anxiety* to describe the baseline condition of mental excitation that maximizes performance. Peak brain growth, they found, is stimulated under conditions that are unstable but still perceived to be manageable. Take, for instance, traveling in a foreign country where one does not speak the language. Life becomes challenging but not completely unmanageable in this case. Neural activity becomes energized by the invited challenge. The brain knows it cannot go on autopilot but, rather, has to learn and therefore seems to find a new gear. The goad to pay attention forces the questing brain to think in new ways and grow.

Yerkes and Dodson's findings continue to be validated by scientific research nearly a century later. As recently as 2018, in a study published by the journal *Neuron*,[5] Daeyeol Lee and his colleagues at Yale University investigated the relationship between uncertainty and learning in rhesus macaque monkeys.

The study involved training the monkeys to play a computer game in which they were shown a series of images and had to select the one that differed from the others. In some trials, the correct answer was always the same, whereas in other trials, the correct answer could vary.

The researchers found that the monkeys were better at learning in conditions of uncertainty, when they had to adapt and adjust their responses based on feedback from previous trials. In these uncertain conditions, the monkeys were able to quickly learn the correct answer and improve their performance over time.

Even more interesting, the researchers used functional magnetic resonance imaging (fMRI) to study the neural activity of the monkeys during the task. They found that certain brain regions, such as the dorsolateral prefrontal cortex, were more active when the monkeys were faced with uncertain conditions, suggesting that these regions play a key role in learning under conditions of uncertainty.

The study has implications for understanding how humans and other animals learn and adapt to changing environments. It suggests uncertainty might be a desirable or even necessary condition for effective learning, and the ability to adapt to uncertainty could be a key component of cognitive flexibility and intelligence.

---

[5]   Bart Massi, Christopher H. Donahue, and Daeyeol Lee, "Volatility Facilitates Value Updating in the Prefrontal Cortex," *Neuron* 99 (August 8, 2018): 598–608.

The paradox of the comfort zone, then, comes alive in the face of major change. First, a sense of mastery can create the misapprehension (as it did with me) that you can "just figure it out" after you take the leap, but that approach runs the risk of pitching you into the panic zone, where learning, growth, and performance are halted or slowed. On the flip side, some measure of change and uncertainty seems to be critical to optimizing for continued cognitive development.

Given this conundrum, what conditions enable someone to use change to their advantage? And what conditions can cause paralysis? In short, a sweeping change, like retirement, is ideally approached incrementally over time, balancing the inherent uncertainty of an unclear future with a sense of relaxed control. If you leap too fast, your brain may well trigger the classic fear responses of fight (overt resistance), flight (denial), or freezing (paralysis). The key is to leverage the benefits of gradual change so your brain can start building new neural pathways in a state of optimal (but not overwhelming) anxiety.

Visualizing the Comfort Zone

There's a simple graphic I use to illustrate the difference between the effects of sudden, overwhelming change and the incremental change that stimulates learning and growth. For starters, I draw a circle on a board. "Here you are, and here's your comfort zone," I point out. "Everything you already have is within this circle; most or all of what you want but don't have is outside it." Judging by the usual display of knowing nods that ensue, I frequently see that my visual strategy rings a bell.

Comfort Zone Diagram

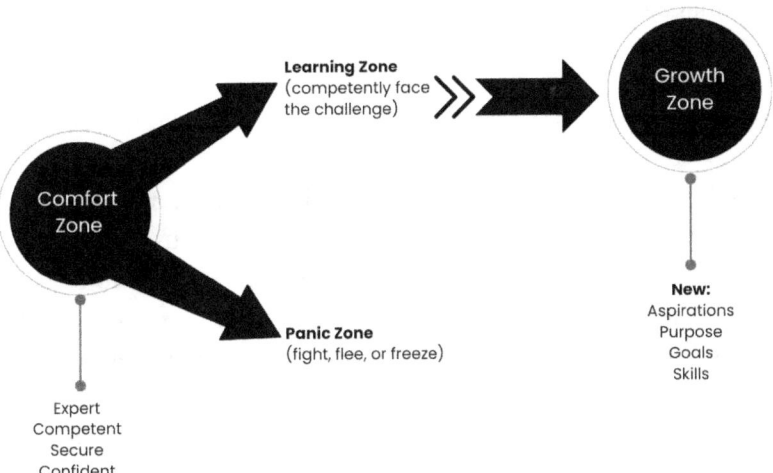

I explain that the comfort zone—where you are before you retire—is the place you feel competent and sure of yourself and understand how you fit into the picture. You know you are skillful and capable. You don't stop and wonder whether you will be able to do what you need to do, contribute how you want to contribute, or have what you wish to have. You're very secure in where you stand. It's what you have been doing for decades. You know how it works, and you're a master of what you need to make happen every day. And even if you need to learn something new, you know how to go about learning it. You're not daunted.

We then consider retirement as the change that will soon force you out of your comfort zone, either suddenly or gradually, depending on how you approach it. As the lower aspect of the diagram shows, if the sudden approach proves to be overwhelming, you might land in the panic zone, where forward progress feels impossible, laden with fear and anxiety, very much like I did. But if you take the incremental approach shown on the upper aspect of the diagram, by building intentional plans for your exit and your approach to new endeavors, you are far more likely to find yourself in the learning and growth zone, where your brain is stimulated to face fresh challenges in a manageable way over time.

The Gentle Glide

This is part of why we help people build toward a new life before they've ended the previous one. There's a term we use with people: "the taper." We counsel them to start the taper a year to eighteen months ahead of their retirement date, and what we mean by that is tapering down the professional work they do as they ramp up the time they're investing in future endeavors and other parts of life. We often chart the taper by defining a steady band of engagement, only with the balance between the old career and the new endeavors steadily shifting in favor of the latter. What the taper allows is a gentle and manageable glide into the future instead of running to the edge of a cliff into the great unknown.

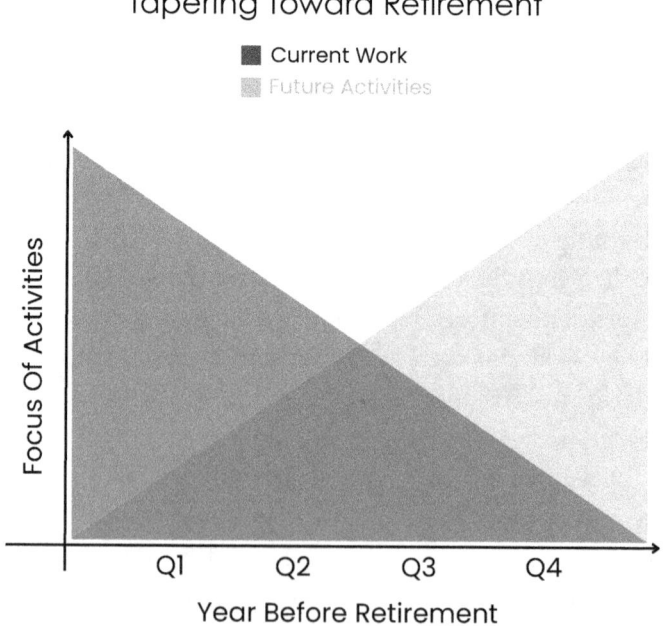

Tapering Toward Retirement

■ Current Work
■ Future Activities

For certain types of people, "base-jumping" out of a career might hold great appeal, even a sense of exhilaration. They may see freedom and possibility in the improvisation. For the group we mostly address ourselves to, the ad lib approach is anathema. Many if not most professionals are risk averse. They prefer to plan. They want to know they're in the driver's seat. They want to feel competent—something they are accustomed to and greatly esteem. To some degree, they will have to adopt the mindset of a student as they embark on their new pursuit. However, the novice haphazardly racing forward—that's not who they are.

Those who work right up to the end, turn off the light switch, and walk out the door rarely have an easy time of it. Not having prepared for retirement, they tend to find themselves walking into a void. The psychology of winging it is extremely risky. As I noted before, we all know people who retire without a plan and enter into a rapid decline. Perhaps one of the most common reasons we hear from our clients for why they have chosen to plan for their postcareer transition is that they are afraid it's the beginning of the end. The fear is existential. *Who am I going to be? Am I even going to be around in five years?*

The Twin Pillars of Intentional Retirement Planning

As I reflected on my own exit from law and the ensuing years-long confusion, I realized I had been engaged in two underlying processes to find new solid ground. First, I needed to rebuild and expand my identity, which had become inextricably intertwined with my role as a lawyer at an elite law firm. Second, because I had lost the entire architecture that shaped how I lived, I needed to design new structures, routines, habits, and metrics to measure progress in my life. As I codified the years of work undergirding my own transition, two critical exercises emerged that form fundamental aspects of our work with clients. The first, which takes a unique look at the enduring aspects of a person's identity, helps our clients reconnect with the parts of themselves they are not losing as they say goodbye to their careers. The second provides a new framework for how to organize life, recognizing that the demands of an intense career will no longer be a defining—or limiting—factor.

In 2019, I read an article by Harvard Business School psychologist Teresa Amabile that astutely described both these processes perfectly. Titled "How Retirement Changes Your Identity," it coincided with her own pending retirement, and it incorporated her and her colleagues' empirical research into psychological shifts that occur leading up to, and during, retirement. Their findings stressed two key processes retirees undergo, termed "identity bridging" and "life restructuring." Amabile's descriptions and conclusions bear out the experience I had personally and have since had with people facing and navigating the changes brought about by retirement. In particular, the study gave ballast to the identity-bridging work we do, premised as it is in recognizing that individuals have existential and enduring parts of themselves, even as they let go of certain context-specific aspects.

I found the piece deeply validating as it reinforced how I approach these twin pillars in my coaching. With gratitude, I will use her terms throughout this book.

Chapter Summary

It is common for intense professionals to become identified with their careers, their firms, or both, which can make the act of retirement feel like an existential threat and create a confusing sense of apprehension.

At any given time, we all occupy a comfort zone, which is a context in which we feel effective, confident, and even masterful. Moving out of our comfort zones can promote learning and growth, provided we manage change in a manner that does not produce paralysis or panic.

Because retirement affects nearly every aspect of life and requires leaving the comfort zone, planning for this monumental change in advance helps leverage the positive aspects of change while avoiding the risks associated with the fear responses of "freeze, fight, or flight."

In our experience, most people benefit from a gradual or tapered approach to winding down their career in parallel with building toward their future, preferably according to an intentional but flexible plan.

There are two primary processes that occur when navigating the change of retirement: identity bridging and life restructuring, which I will address in Parts Two and Three, respectively.

PART TWO

IDENTITY CRISIS

Who Will I Be if I'm Not What I Do?

chapter four

A SHORT BIOGRAPHY OF A TOTAL SUCCESS

In the social jungle of human existence,
there is no feeling of being alive without a sense of identity.

~ Erik Erikson, psychologist

Becoming Howard Marks

The story I tell here represents a portmanteau of several talented and successful individuals whom I have had the privilege to guide as they developed their plans for life in retirement. Understandably, because retiring from their luminary careers presented its existential challenges, they have elected not to offer their names as a matter of privacy, which I thoroughly respect. Nevertheless, their individual and collective postcareer triumphs are spectacular, especially when juxtaposed with the sense of confusion that accompanied the idea of losing their identities as highly successful and prominent professionals. Please accept this narrative as illustrative of the key themes that make their particular stories so compelling and know that the individuals who have inspired this portmanteau are living truly inspired lives in their postcareer chapters.

Howard Marks gave thirty-five years of his life to the multibillion-dollar law firm he had worked for his entire career. He joined its Chicago office in 1985 and within six years was elected to partnership. In 2002, he ushered in the new millennium by becoming the global chair of the firm's corporate department, and for more than a decade, his successes would map the boundaries of influence across the firm, with reward loops and strategic relationships at every turn. Not only did Howard advise blue chip companies on transactional matters, but he also had a hand in steering business decisions at the firm.

Then came a leadership change. The managing partner retired after a long and influential run. He and Howard had shared a special bond and tremendous mutual respect. Howard suddenly found himself edging toward a career precipice. On paper, the Yale magna cum laude and Harvard Law School JD had scaled the zenith of his field—ranked consistently as a leading corporate lawyer by *The Legal 500 US* and as Band 1 by *Chambers USA*. In practice, though, he felt his relevance slipping and his overall satisfaction beginning to wane.

Another year and then another elapsed as his birthdays came and went. Younger blood now swarmed the power rungs, and their own clients also wanted to work with fresher faces. As the phone went increasingly silent, so too the invitations to participate in this meeting or that event dropped off. Howard's self-perception of becoming irrelevant did not take shape overnight. He continued to feel he was as fit to contribute as ever. But with time, he could no longer deny the mounting signs that the reality around him had changed. As with all successful professionals, his clout had an expiration date, and that date was fast approaching if it was not already there. At age sixty, he seemed to be slowly but inexorably aging out.

Howard's firm wasn't deliberately eclipsing its erstwhile nova. Making room for new talent is how such a planetary body survives.

Yet the dimming of Howard's star power was no less concerning for being the natural order of things. Finally, Howard talked to the executive committee and gave them twelve months' notice. Suddenly, retirement became "a real thing," he recounted.

When Howard met with us, he was visibly troubled. What had been a dazzling career seemed to be ending on a darker note for him. He had helped build the firm. He had been a culture bearer. He prized his experiences in both practice and management. "I am not someone who spent my career counting down the days to retirement," he explained. He had loved his career and had enjoyed too much positivity to flame out with a negative charge.

Naturally, he was feeling conflicted about it all. Adding to his tension was the fact that he thrives on human interaction and collaboration, loves embracing fresh challenges, and enjoys encouraging others to do the same. He could not imagine who he would be or what his life would be like without these oxygen sources.

Howard came to us on the brink of big losses. He was losing his colleagues. He was losing his professional purpose. He was losing his community. He was losing his self-image as a highly successful lawyer and partner at one of the world's top law firms. In his eyes, Howard's retirement seemed to spell the end of Howard. It was no secret to him that he had become highly identified with his career and related achievements. But he was thoroughly perplexed as to how he would extricate himself from this deep sense of career identification.

I Achieve; Therefore, I Am

Howard's enmeshment with his career was nothing new to us. Nearly every professional we meet expresses some form of identification with working life. I remember quite clearly one of our clients expressing it this way: "I achieve; therefore, I am. So exactly who will I be as a retired guy?"

Think about the last time you were asked to introduce yourself to a group of people. You probably began with the major roles you play in life. For most intense professionals in North America, that almost always includes our self-described métier: "I'm a lawyer"; "I'm an investment banker"; "I'm a CEO"; "I'm an accountant." We often then provide clarifying details about that professional role by elaborating on where we work, our specialty, or our level in our organization. If pressed, we might then share information about our personal roles: "I'm a mother of two"; "I'm married with three daughters"; "my partner and I split our time between DC and New York."

Then there's the exercise of drafting a CV or bio. We summarize our work experience, our education, our recognitions, and our accomplishments. These details provide a set of facts to help others make sense of who we are, how they might relate to us, and where we fit into the bigger picture with them.

All this is perfectly normal and necessary. These aspects of ourselves provide narrative and color to the complex question of who we are and what our lives have been and continue to be about. Without defining and sharing them, we would struggle to see how and where we fit. We would miss opportunities to join groups, connect with others, and perceive our personal progress toward the goals and objectives we have set for ourselves.

The challenge, however, is that we forget we have an authentic and enduring self beneath the roles, successes, and achievements. Were we not "someone" before we graduated from the elite university? Before we married and had children? Before we were promoted to partner? Before we became president of the national nonprofit organization?

The answer is "Of course," but putting a finger on what that elusive self is in the absence of the external roles and successes is challenging indeed. And if you cannot locate yourself beyond those component parts, then the loss of them can feel as threatening as death itself.

The Psychology of Motivation

As I began to unwind my own Gordian knot of self and career, I discovered how my subconscious motivations had played a significant role in my predicament. Digging into the psychology of motivation revealed some important clues. While I am no psychologist, and there are almost certainly more complexities to the matter than my layman's research uncovered, I found the following information extremely helpful. In my survey of the psychological studies on motivation, I uncovered three important motivational properties of the self:

1. Communion
2. Agency
3. Coherence

Overall, these three motivational properties are interconnected and work together to promote well-being and positive functioning. When people feel a sense of communion, agency, and coherence, they are more likely to feel fulfilled and satisfied with their lives. With that in mind, I could begin to see how my career had enabled me to satisfy each of these needs, thereby creating critical anchors in terms of how I organized my sense of who I was and how I fit into the world. When I share these insights with my clients, inevitably, they begin to see why they feel identified with their professional lives.

Let's start with communion. The human animal has herding tendencies that make us seek out connection and belonging. Social creatures that we are, we want to feel a bond with other people and that we belong somewhere. Our second organizing property, agency, gives us a sense of autonomy and competence, so we are skilled and empowered to make things happen. We know what to do to achieve desired results, providing a feeling of control over our life and a sense of self-determination. Which brings us to property number three, coherence. This speaks to our desire to have a clear and consistent sense of self—for regularity, predictability, and routine. Our need for coherence explains why we're forever looking to establish macro, or even micro, patterns so we don't have to constantly manage internal or external chaos. Fending off instability is a very exhausting thing for a human being to do. To preempt such a fate, we create routines and feel best when we know what is expected of us and what to expect from the world around us. A measure of predictability helps ground us, it seems.

When you think about it, work and career, particularly among successful professionals, serve up a healthy response to all three motivating impulses. Lawyers, for example, belong to a profession or a cohort of exceedingly high-functioning people. Those who work at a law firm also belong to an even tighter ring of the professional community. Being part of a local office and even a team provides a sense of belonging somewhere with other people who operate like you do and who have your back. Yet with retirement, all that goes out the window. There goes the occupational family that has helped satisfy the need for communion.

And what happens to the sense of agency? By the time retirement is looming, most people have a great deal of agency and autonomy—they make big decisions; they lead important matters; they know how to solve problems that others don't. Over the course of a career, they have become highly capable in their roles, probably a true expert. That competence can feel practically irrelevant once the career ends.

Now what about coherence? A long tenure in working life has provided a structure that creates pattern and routine. What makes me get out of bed every morning? What are the repeating themes and rhythms of my days and weeks, and how do they fit in my life? People say, "For forty years I get up and do my exercises, commute, and then I'm at work all day, and I leave at seven o'clock, and I come home." Those patterns are enormously ingrained. The mantra we hear in one form or another is "I know how to do the things I'm doing, I know who I'm going to be doing them with, and I know when and where to show up. That's my life, and it makes sense to me."

Stripped down to the core, coherence creates the sense of "right place, right time." Recognizing that retirement causes a major disturbance to one's sense of coherence underscores the importance of intentionally building a new game plan for daily and weekly rhythms, habits, and routines after the press of career no longer imposes them.

When I point out to clients that retirement upends one of their major sources of communion, agency, and coherence, it helps them realize they're not crazy to find this change unsettling. Considering the bulwarks of identity that stand to be toppled, it's clear why the prospect of retiring can feel so difficult. This insight also highlights why plenty of advance planning for retirement is essential to recreate sources for these properties in life. The leaping-off-the-cliff model appears all the riskier considering the existential needs that must be requited moving forward. Without a thoughtful design, starting over can be a deeply dislocating experience.

The Shifting Sands of Purpose

Many of the men and women who seek out our coaching are grappling with major life questions as they approach retirement, not the least of which is their future purpose. As they ascended the rungs of their profession, they were also raising families, paying off homes, and solving other immediate challenges. The demands of middle adulthood tend to give us a built-in purpose centered around providing for our families, striving for financial security, and building a foundation that will endure over time. Working life is often driven by the desire to establish these things, and our purpose is thus fueled. But for most at the end of a successful career, they're no longer scratching their heads and wondering how they will pay for college or the next family vacation. Having fully satisfied the drive to survive and provide, the questions start to tilt into the existential realm. *Why am I here?* for example. *If I no longer need to work, what will get me out of bed in the morning?* Ironically, the very drive for success that energized their sense of purpose, once fulfilled, seems to be robbing them of it. And for many, as I noted before, the idea of a permanent vacation is clearly not the answer.

Psychologist Viktor Frankl famously wrote,

> Mental health is based on a certain degree of tension, the tension between what one has already achieved and what one still ought to accomplish, or the gap between what one is and what one should become. . . . What man actually needs is not a tensionless state but rather the striving and struggling for a worthwhile goal, a freely chosen task.[6]

Frankl's observation captures perfectly what many of our clients know in their guts—without a renewed purpose that gives their lives a sense of meaning, they are at risk for decline in every way.

I often turn to the work of Abraham Maslow to shed light on how the end of a successful career correlates with an evolution in purpose. Maslow was an American psychologist best known for describing the hierarchy of needs as a driver of human behavior. His theory posits that human needs are organized in a hierarchy, with the most basic needs at the bottom and higher needs at the top. In brief, Maslow's five levels of needs are:

---

[6] Frankl, Viktor E. *Man's Search for Meaning*, 1946.

Maslow's Hierarchy of Needs

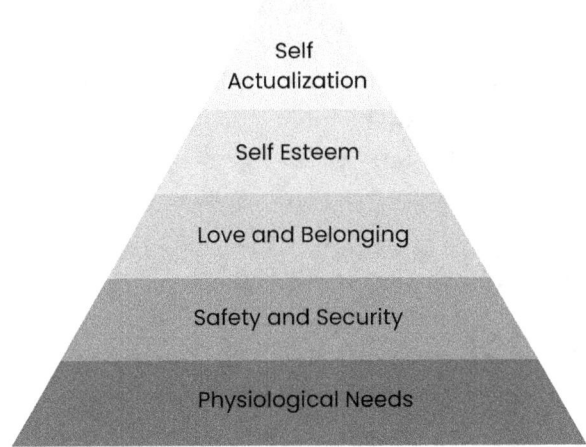

According to Maslow, individuals must first meet their basic physiological and safety needs before they can move up to focus on the higher needs of love and belonging, esteem, and, finally, self-actualization. In his book *Motivation and Personality*, he described this dynamic as "the full use and exploitation of talents, capacities, potentialities, etc." Otherwise put, individuals are constantly striving to attain greater levels of well-being and creativity in an effort to reach their fullest potential. Importantly, Maslow saw self-actualization as an ongoing process, not as an endpoint or a destination.

One of the characteristics he believed to be fundamental in self-actualizing people was the ability to have peak experiences. Why wouldn't a retired person just want to sit on the beach all day slurping a piña colada? Maslow tells us a life of idle leisure flattens the space for self-discovery. Such a droning existence offers the very opposite of the upward stretch toward a heightened sense of purpose.

Figuring out what that new purpose might be, then, is part of the deal. With the basic needs of survival and security met and with the experience of competence and accomplishment acquired over a successful career, one might now ask, *What else am I capable of? What else is there to discover about my potential?* As one lawyer put it after he had been retired for a couple of years,

> You have to ask yourself what the return on investment is to spend one more year doing what you've been doing for forty years, when you've earned the money you need and you've achieved all that you hoped to, versus spending that same year working on the next chapter of your life.

Maslow would have been nodding vigorously.

The brink of retirement may be the first time in a long time most people are being invited to take a broader look at themselves, to explore with curiosity their own fresh interests and aspirations. Years of unrelenting demands have buffered them from these questions, and this new territory can be as liberating as it is intimidating. There's a dual challenge in store: to acknowledge and appreciate the tremendous growth and accomplishment that has already occurred but also to sit with the question of what else is possible in terms of growth, potential, and opportunity.

A Whole New Life Stage

To complicate matters further, as the external change of retirement rears its head, our clients are often entering a new stage of life, psychologically speaking. Many imagine that an inexorable burnout has finally overtaken their motivation, but we offer an alternative explanation to consider.

Jeremy was a name brand in the private equity space who enlisted our guidance in 2017. We know what burnout looks like, and Jeremy, though barely pushing sixty, appeared to be feeling its effects. But we suspected there was more to his story than met the eye.

The senior partner had essentially built his firm's private equity practice from the ground up. At the time, private equity was a fairly new concept in law firms, with few believing it could amount to much. But Jeremy believed. For him, the prospect of amassing funds from diverse portfolio companies, each of which would need legal tending, smacked of promise. The seer was also a doer, and over the subsequent decades, he was extremely instrumental in shaping his idea into one of the firm's most successful groups.

But now, Jeremy was confused by his attitude toward his work. He said, "I feel anxious because what I used to be able to do now feels nearly impossible." He furnished a ready example.

> I always sleep with my phone next to my bed because my clients are so demanding. Well, a couple of weeks ago, my phone rings at one in the morning. It's a private equity fund manager, and he's barking in my ear, "I need you to turn this document around, and I need it on my desk by seven a.m." Incidentally, this guy is probably twenty-six years old. So I put on my jogging suit and sneakers and trudge down to the office. When I get there, thank goodness, there's a younger colleague working at his desk. He sees me and says, "Jeremy, I'll take care of this for you; go back to bed. This is what I'm here to do. You're a senior partner." So I'm walking home thinking to myself, *This is a young man's game.* But at the same time, I'm also thinking, *I'm not even that old.*

That was the moment Jeremy understood he couldn't continue his Ironman push. "I used to be energized by the idea that my input was needed so urgently," he recalled. "I had to be able to perform on point and at the top of my game, whether it was one in the afternoon or one in the morning. Just knowing I could do it was rewarding for me." That was then. Now the thought that tweaked his psyche was very different. It alerted him that working with private equity clients was an extreme sport he no longer cared to play.

What made Jeremy's story especially poignant was his frank expression of confusion. "I don't know if it means that I really am done working, or if I just need to take a break," he shared. But what he recognized was that he could no longer keep redlining at peak intensity and expect a positive outcome.

A mind in flux obeys its own tempo. So I waited for a breather before interpreting his inner drama. "You have just teed up the perfect example of an issue that everybody around your age is confronting," I noted. "And it tends to happen at the very turning point in the life cycle when the world says to retire."

Without any warning, Jeremy had stepped into a new phase of adulthood. His psychology was developing right on schedule, despite his oblivion to it. Jeremy would need to revisit his old assumptions and construct new ones for the stage he was entering. To align his expectations with his emotions, I reached into my conceptual tool kit. "This is where a psychological framework is important," I asserted, positioning him to appreciate the broader picture. The turmoil he was grappling with wasn't just some burnout. Rather, as I explained, it was an inner psychological shift that happened to coincide with the external inflection point of retirement.

The framework Jeremy was introduced to that day borrows from the German-born developmental psychologist and psychoanalyst Erik Erikson. Erikson is known for identifying eight stages of psychosocial development, with each stage in his model corresponding to certain core strengths, drivers, relationships, and fears. The elements of this apparatus help us organize ourselves and achieve a sense of psychological and social well-being.

The first six stages occur early in life, so they're not terribly relevant to our cohort. The latter two, however, are extremely instructive for people who fall into the age categories we guide.

Stage seven of Erikson's chart—what he calls "middle adulthood"—is marked by a need to contribute and work at the level of one's potential. In this stage, we are motivated to figure out what we are capable of and make a go of it—in a word, to succeed. Whether raising a family or building a career, our driver is to do meaningful contributive work that is a match to our abilities. Our core relationships during this stage tend to be our close family, our community, and our colleagues, spanning a fairly tight circle of human beings. Our biggest fear in middle adulthood is not living up to our potential and ending up "unsuccessful" in our own view. That period of life in Erikson's model runs from age forty to age sixty or sixty-five.

For Jeremy, learning about the sequences of psychosocial development proved revelatory. He had already been noticing for some time that he was no longer driven by the same motives as before, just as he had been feeling that his ability to show up in a similarly intense way was flagging. "Well, that's because you're stepping into late adulthood," I informed him. He looked at me like I had just cracked dark matter. So I continued.

As you enter late adulthood, your core strength goes from "production and care" to "wisdom," and your core driver goes from working like hell in the chase for success to synthesizing meaning and understanding what the nature of your contributions in middle adulthood added up to. Your core relationships expand from that close circle of human beings to all mankind. You start to figure out where you fit in the grand scheme of things. Earlier, your biggest fear was not living up to your potential, but in late adulthood, your biggest fear is feeling like your life has been meaningless, as if you leaned your ladder against the wrong building, climbed to the top, and went, *Why did I do that?* This is what leads to bitterness and cynicism in later life.

The effects of my Erikson explanation were tangibly felt by Jeremy. He said, "Yes! That describes exactly what I've been experiencing, and I had no idea what to make of it. I did not know it was a fairly normal shift." Jeremy went from thinking, *Something is wrong with me* to thinking, *Oh, I'm just entering a new stage of my life.*

Significantly, one of the results of our work was a value-etched clarity of purpose. Jeremy pronounced his newfound conviction with both an embrace of and a breaking with the past. The words he chose to express this were memorable: "It's been really fun building this practice, but I have to say, I'm no longer interested in helping rich people get richer." As for the critical Eriksonian step of reflection, his observation was, "I really want to take the knowledge I've learned, the relationships I've built, and the skills I've honed and figure out a way to have a big impact."

One idea we came up with pointed him in a particularly auspicious direction. We were inquiring about organizations he admires, and he mentioned the Robin Hood Foundation. The brainchild of Paul Tudor Jones, a hedge fund billionaire, the foundation's creation story got Jeremy thinking. Tudor Jones had pulled together the resources of hedge fund industry insiders to cover operating expenses so the foundation could give grants to the twenty most effective nonprofits in New York City trying to raise people out of poverty.

Jeremy recapped that impressive history and said,

> Well, I can do the same thing in the private equity sphere. I know how to form funds. I know how to pull people's money together for focused purposes. I have all these relationships in the private equity world, so why don't I think about bringing them together in a Robin Hood–type foundation—but with private equity firms instead of hedge funds?

Jeremy's broad focus would be human rights, starting with immigration justice.

It was vindicating to see Jeremy embrace the recognition that giving back was what would inspire him going forward. Working hard would not. Jeremy underwent an internal shift. He hadn't previously grasped what was going on with him. He had always been very proud of his ability to work hard and of his drive to do so. When that started fading, he felt lost and confused. Now he was realizing that this heightened vulnerability was a normal unfolding of life in a psychosocial sequence that pretty much everyone experiences. Once embraced, the future can be imagined differently from the past.

It is common for our clients to struggle to figure out what the future looks like because they only know the past. They only know what it's like to work like a demon and have their validation be largely a product of how well they're able to do that.

Jeremy's big *aha* moment was as sudden as it was profound. "I get it now—I just need a whole new set of measures and a whole new way of framing what I'm good at," he enthused. "And the ability to share my wisdom in service of having a positive impact and seeing that everything I've done up to this point has meaning that I can translate into something I care about. That's my work now."

For Jeremy, getting the dead-of-night phone call was his moment of clarity. It's when he realized, *This is no longer energizing me. What am I doing?* By the same token, for his thirty-three-year-old colleague, being a dynamo working by the midnight oil was just fine. That's what he was there to do at this stage of his life.

Chapter Summary

Intense career professionals tend to conflate who they are with what they do and what they have achieved.

Because working life has provided a primary engine for productivity, accomplishment, and recognition, it can be difficult to imagine how to stay relevant and contributive after an intense career.

Understanding how one's profession helps answer their core motivational desires for communion, agency, and coherence is important to designing new ways to meet those needs.

As retirement approaches, many people notice they need to embrace a shifting purpose—from engaging in work that builds the foundations of relationships and financial security to determining what is yet possible in terms of their continued growth and contribution.

On top of the need to redefine how we meet the motivational properties of the self and to reconstruct our purpose, retirement often coincides with the transition from middle adulthood to late adulthood, when our psychological drivers, strengths, relationships, and fears are changing internally.

When so many core satisfiers of an individual's purpose and motivation are disturbed at once, it can be difficult to see new pathways for growth and meaning. Yet these elements are vital to staying fully alive.

chapter five

BEYOND THE BIO—WHO ARE YOU?

Inside us there is something that has no name, that something is what we are.

~ José Saramago

Getting a Handle on the Self

Identity. The foundation of our work surrounding retirement investigates the question of who we really are under the roles we play in work and life. The mystery of self-concept is among the mind's earliest dilemmas. It led the ancients to theorize how humans come to know their emotions, impulses, and relative strengths, and the elusive nature of this mental process kept philosophers plenty busy throughout medieval times. How the conception of the self evolved is a tale for another book. Here, we'll leapfrog over centuries of thinkers—over René Descartes, over Sigmund Freud, over self-theorists Prescott Lecky and Victor Raimy—and alight on the mid-twentieth-century notions advanced by humanistic psychologists like Carl Rogers and Michael Lewis. What can they teach us about self-concept, how it comes to exist, and how it evolves over time?

Carl Rogers believed that self-concept is central to understanding human behavior and psychological well-being. According to Rogers, the self-concept is composed of three components:

1. Self-image
2. Self-esteem
3. Self-ideal

Self-image is the way we see ourselves in terms of physical appearance, personality traits, and other specific personal characteristics. Self-esteem is the degree to which we value and accept ourselves based on our self-image. The self-ideal is our perception of who we most aspire to be or become. Our view of the gap between our self-image and our ideal self can influence our self-esteem and overall self-concept, positively or negatively. Further, when our self-concept is affirming and congruent with our experiences, we are more likely to have positive feelings about ourselves and the world around us. In contrast, when our self-concept is negative or incongruent with our experiences, we may experience feelings of anxiety, depression, or other emotional distress.

As Rogers posited and humanistic psychology continues to affirm, a positive self-concept is necessary for psychological health and well-being. It becomes important, then, for us to consider how approaching retirement might affect our self-image, self-esteem, and overall self-concept, unless we can see a future that enhances these things instead of diminishing them.

In 1990, Michael Lewis helpfully distinguished between two main aspects of the self-concept: the existential self and the categorical self. For our purposes, we like to use "existential identity" and "categorical identity." I'll explain. Existential identity encompasses the characteristics that we understand to be separate, distinct, and, most importantly, *enduring* about ourselves. These are not contingent characteristics, but rather what we consider to be fundamental to who we always were and always will be. Which is not to say these attributes are static; a better way to describe them is consistent. In my case, five of these are *I'm a woman. I'm a nurturing person. I'm curious. I like to explore. I'm an optimist.* We don't often consciously think about the components of our existential identity because they are so embedded in our sense of who we are.

Categorical identity, on the other hand, has to do with the categories we join or feel we belong to. Otherwise put, it gets at the malleable or more transient aspects of our identities, such as traits, skills, roles we play in life, or professions we assume. For example, "I'm a parent." "I'm a partner in this law firm." "I'm the president of this club." These are ephemeral aspects or roles that can come and go throughout a lifetime. We will delve into the importance of our relationship to the roles we play in chapter 6. For now, note that we all categorize ourselves in important ways to bolster our sense of belonging, which naturally feeds into our self-concept.

With these discernments in mind, let's reexamine the very picture of success, Howard, and the psychological impact of his impending retirement. Howard's self-concept was heavily defined by his professional life. His membership in his prestigious law firm community aligned powerfully with his self-image as a highly capable and responsive individual who could deliver superior results under pressure. His self-esteem was continually enhanced by his performance and validated by positive feedback and robust compensation. The idea that he would soon lose this rarified position along with his platform for exercising his skills and abilities understandably left him reeling. Conscious of the reason or not, Howard quietly dreaded his retirement because it seemed to spell the end of a hard-won self-concept with nowhere to go. It became crucial, therefore, for Howard to connect with the aspects of his self-concept that would continue, regardless of the change in his working life.

Uncovering What Endures

As we explored in chapter 3, change can stimulate growth and learning, provided that it is managed in a way that does not cause panic or paralysis. Further, as thinkers like Frankl and Maslow professed, humans are wired for continued growth and need to discover fresh sources of challenge and meaning to feel energized and alive. Retirement, then, seems to offer a magnificent opportunity, as long as we equip ourselves to navigate this journey beyond merely confirming our bank balance.

One of the most critical aspects of our work with clients is reconnecting them consciously with their existential identities, or the parts of themselves that will endure and grow regardless of the constancy of their professional life. For the person who is on the road to retirement, the impending loss of their key defining role can feel like an approaching avalanche that will sweep all else along with it. *There goes my entire self in the transformation*, the fear seems to rumble underfoot. Being able to see the next phase as change amid continuity is an important step toward trusting they can preserve their footing on solid ground.

In facilitating a client's description of their enduring self, we deconstruct the overarching question of *Who are you?* into a number of manageable pieces, which together provide an organized way to view the lasting aspects of oneself. As we often say, "You cannot see the picture when you are in the picture." This process helps our clients step out of their pictures to get a perspective on who they really are and will continue to be, regardless of where and how they work. And it all starts with stories and what we can uncover as they are told in real time.

As a child, I devoured books. I would go to the library with my dad on a Saturday and check out fifteen books, read them all week, then return the next Saturday for fifteen more. I loved story. Even in my law practice, what I was most fascinated by were my clients and colleagues. This made me a bit of an oddball. I was a little out of step with the rest of my colleagues because I was so interested in the human side of everything. The technical work engaged the part of my brain that solved jigsaws, but I was really all about the people and wanting to understand them.

I suppose part of leaving my career was about finding my ultimate calling. Law was definitely an area in which I performed with excellence—but genius? What I'm uniquely suited to do? No. On some level, I used the legitimate excuse of needing more time with my family and extricated myself from a profession that felt like a mismatch to my true purpose.

To earn a living initially, I worked as a recruiter for lawyers who were changing careers or firms. More and more, I found myself weaving storytelling into our discussions. *Tell me about you. Tell me what matters to you. Why are you leaving this firm? What's working? What isn't? What would be ideal at the next place?* The "tell me a story" approach is native to who I am, even if recruiting was just a stepping stone on my own path to reinvention.

Then came the economic collapse of 2008, which thankfully spelled the end of my recruiting stint, which had started to feel boring. The legal market contracted, and I knew lots of lawyers were going to be catapulted out of their firms with nowhere to go. Recalling my own struggle when I exited my legal career, I decided to codify my reinvention efforts of the prior five years and create a program to meet the current moment. In order to resonate with intense professionals, its value proposition would have to account for their most prized resource—time. One thing intense career professionals never have enough of is time. The slightest hint that you are going to waste it will activate their combative reflexes. I asked myself, *What is the quickest and most efficient approach to help path seekers identify their essential values and purpose?* From here, my own new professional life was born.

Identity-Bridging Fundamentals: Why? How? What Else?

As we use story to explore the enduring aspects of the self, our clients can start to see the supporting piers of the bridge that will carry them from their current self-concept to a future identity that makes sense yet feels fresh. Answering the questions of why we do what we do, how we make hard things happen, and what else we still want to experience or accomplish is pivotal to the process.

A common opening salvo I'll lob is "Tell me a story of a time when you felt that you were engaged in a way that you really shine, and somebody else was getting a great benefit?" I may riff a little more to ease the person into the groove: "You experienced that reward loop where you felt you were on purpose, in the zone, doing your thing."

The storytelling begins, and I'm listening for themes. Normally, I will follow up with a request for two or three more stories because I want to hear one that's set in their professional world, one that's drawn from their personal life, and one that reflects their social dynamics. Together, we are building an anthology of first-person oral history. "Take me back in time," I tell them. In that sense, I am a character detective, and they are leaving behind a trail of hints. Each story carries an element of suspense as I sleuth out the dead giveaway that is deeply thematic for this individual. The investigative method I use for these "whydunnits" centers around careful listening. As they're talking, I'm taking notes. When I feel that a motivational theme is starting to cohere, I craft a sentence that captures it. I'll then say something like, "This is what I think I'm hearing. But I want you to read this sentence, and if it does not resonate with you, out it goes." Usually what ensues is a combination of delight and mystification. They'll announce, "That's it exactly! But how did you get it?" The next step is to edit the sentence. Or, in the event that it fails to land, we will throw it out and start over. We will do whatever it takes to get it right.

We asked Peggy Davenport (whom we met in chapter 1) to remember instances when she felt she was showing up in a very natural way, using a real strength, and somebody else was getting an obvious benefit. The first story she conveyed brought her back to an electronic platform she'd created at her law firm—long before the era of chat rooms—where women could share concerns and practical advice about raising kids and managing the demands of working life. Informally dubbed "the park bench," it blossomed into an affinity group, replete with guest speakers and mentoring opportunities, that earned the moniker the Women's Resource Group. "It was a space for women at the firm to be with other women and grow from that experience and feel safe there," she reminisces.

An additional remembrance she relayed came up in the values analysis associated with her animating purpose. This story had to do with encouraging her friends to get into endurance sports. "I got a whole bunch of girls to do this thing called Ragnar race where you run all night. One of them hadn't even run before." Next, when it came to triathlons, "Another friend learned to run, and another went on to become a nationally ranked triathlete," she recalls.

For Peggy, because her intuitive and intellectual skills are equally off the chart, we divined two "animating purposes." The twin threads we pulled from Peggy's stories blended the strengths of her emotional and rational brains. Later in this book, we'll consider additional factors that helped us unpick the strands, but here, the specific statements we designed will prove illustrative.

The first sentence we came up with for Peggy illustrates how we dynamically connect the dots of the self: "I use my intuition to make authentic choices that expand opportunities for others." Her jaw dropped when I read it. She felt it was so true it was uncanny.

Because she was in a leadership role at her firm, she described stories in which she spotted nonobvious opportunities for people to do certain things. Peggy just knew in her gut that the opportunity was the right thing for that person to do. Again and again, what was motivating her choices was the fact that she knew she would be opening doors for others to succeed.

This brings us to the second sentence we constructed for her: "I use my ability to connect and communicate, to provide security and support so that others can achieve and expand." This sentence drew on the stories she was telling about her ability to be very present and connected with people and to give them something of a safe space so they could unblock themselves from whatever was standing in the way of them fulfilling their potential.

The heart of our work is to discover what feels essentially purposeful to people—the "why" underneath their most inspired and inspiring moments. As we considered new ways for Peggy to live her animating purpose, we entertained a couple of ideas. One involved mentoring young professional women and another serving as a branding or business coach to emerging artists. As we dug into what most matters to Peggy and how she can use her core skills, we came up with a very different idea, one that would potentially allow her to be a huge contributor to the civic well-being of her new universe. That's when it occurred to us that foundation work could be spot-on for her because foundation stakeholders are required to make discerning choices that elevate possibility.

"We've been thinking about it, and we believe you might really enjoy serving on the board of a community foundation," we told Peggy as our session drew to a close. She leaned her head to the side and smiled in abashed bemusement. "I was like, I'm sorry, how do you spell that? I don't know what I thought foundation work was, if I thought about it at all," Peggy reminisces.

"There's a foundation in Jackson Hole that dispenses funds to local causes," we started in. She listened with growing interest as we sketched out the richness of purpose, variety, and social engagement a role with such a foundation could offer. The more we talked, the more she could see that her intuitive skills would enable her to evaluate the people and potential behind each proposed mission while her business and data-crunching skills would also serve her well. Yet a community board in a place like Jackson Hole is usually highly selective; by all expectations, it would be populated by people who are very connected to the community. Nevertheless, we had planted a seed that'd find fertile ground to take root. Peggy reminisces:

> So we move to Jackson Hole. And here my husband Kirk is all booked up already. I've got nothing going on, really, but I start meeting people. One of them is the president of the Community Foundation, and we kind of hit it off. And she says, "I really think you might like to get involved in our competitive grants program. Would that be of interest to you?" Had you not planted the idea that foundation work could be a good fit for me, I don't think my lunch with this woman would have gone anywhere. I would have been like, "No, thank you, I don't do foundation work." But I was more open minded as a result of our session. So, my attitude was *Let's keep talking and see what this is about.* One thing led to another, and now I'm on the board, super active. It's a big part of my life. I just finished a term as the chairperson of Jackson Hole Public Art, which was also a big part of my life.

The community foundation was of a kind with Peggy's animating purpose. It empowered her to make intuitive choices about where the foundation should give its money in order to have the greatest impact or, as the first sentence couched it, to "expand opportunities for others." An important thread that runs through our work is trying to help people get to the guts of what it is they're on this planet to do so they can go do more of it if they've begun or begin doing it if not.

In the telling of her stories, Peggy's "how" also came to life. Collectively, we realized what guided her decision-making. She always made her decisions intuitively, and then she validated them intellectually. She is extremely strong in both of those realms. Yet Peggy had never realized how much she relied on intuition as a first principle and how precisely on point it was for her. Reflecting back on this moment, Peggy recalls:

> When you told me that, I was like, "No, no, no, you don't understand—I am a J on the Myers-Briggs!" Everything is organized and planned out with me. I have very strong executive functioning skills. You were like, "No, you're actually an intuitive decision-maker," and then you gave multiple examples of big decisions in my life where I listened, gathered information, and once I decided to move, I did so very rapidly and assuredly. I'll never forget your telling me, "Our advice is that you not plan your retirement. You don't know what kind of space you're going to be in. You don't know what's going to resonate with you. And you're not yet in the environment of being a retired person. So wait and do your thing, which is intuitive decision-making." I never would have guessed that.
>
> Meanwhile, I had all these lists of everything that I wanted to be in life and was asking which I should start pursuing. Your response was, "Get rid of all of that, and just go out and start living and see what happens." Conversely, about my husband, Kirk, who makes big leaps and jumps and comes off as a little freer and more impulsive than I do, you explained, "He needs a little more of a plan, or it'll be too crazy." With him, you said, "You need to get going, Kirk; you need to make these phone calls; you need to have these meetings." And he's like,

"Wait, why did she get to be the intuitive one while I have a task list?" That was exactly the opposite of what we might have guessed had we not done the program with you.

Peggy's updates during the two years we worked together revealed that she was loving it. The crux of her reflections was surprised gratification.

I cannot believe how seamlessly I've adjusted. I never would have thought of pursuing foundation work. Because I was a private equity lawyer, I wouldn't have understood why I made sense for this role, or why it made sense for me.

Reflecting on what was particularly effective about our approach, she says:

You never cornered me with "What do you want to do in life?" or "What are your values and priorities?" Had you asked that type of question, I think I would have come up with very boring, superficial answers. Instead, you had me do exercises or games that were really intriguing and engrossing, such that I didn't even know what we were doing.

Peggy's story also offers an instructive example of how we explore what else is possible in terms of personal growth and aspiration—the self-ideal I described earlier. All these years later, Peggy still remembers our warm-up of having her name three people she admired. "So I say Barack Obama." She smiles. "And why do you admire Barack Obama?" Peggy recalls us following up.

And I say, "Well, because he's just so sexy." (*Anything else?*) He is a fantastic athlete. (*Can you give me anything else?*) You know, he's very trustworthy and responsible and loyal. (*And who's your next person?*) My husband? (*Okay, why do you like your husband?*) He's really sexy.

Peggy recollects thinking what must have been going through my mind at this point: that I'm "going to have to teach her to be a pole dancer." Joking aside, she wonders why she wasn't saying Mother Teresa or Eleanor Roosevelt.

Why was I talking about sexy guys and athletes with good values? And the answer really was right there, which is that I was going to pivot in a different direction that'd be more of a sensual, athletic life where I would be using my body more. Nonetheless, I wanted to be around people whose values I admired and resonated with my own, such as loyalty and trustworthiness.

Peggy observes that she is no longer defining life by old terms, like "What do you do?" "Where do you work?" "What's your title?" Rather, Peggy observes:

These things are by no means my identity or how I place myself in the world these days, though I'm very grateful to be involved and to contribute. That's the evolution. On the Enneagram personality test, I used to be a Type Three. By nature, I'm an achiever, so that's always going to be there a little bit. But I have moved past defining myself by my achievements. I've become an avid golfer. In golf, you have a handicap, and you play tournaments, and you

win, or you don't. There's a lot of achievement orientation to that sport, which is also the case with a
lot of my hobbies. It's been hard work not to let that
be how I live in the world. But the really cool thing
about retirement is abandoning all of that in favor
of things like spirituality and kindness, mindfulness
and compassion, creativity and exploration.

Peggy is a powerful example of someone whose existential identity grounded her as she developed new and expanded ways to
understand herself.

Rediscovering Play

The idea of play does not get much airtime in the professional arena.
And yet, extensive research makes clear that engaging in play is
both critical to brain development and something we all do to some
degree throughout our lives, even if we call it something else. As
Dr. Stuart Brown, author of *Play: How It Shapes the Brain, Opens
the Imagination, and Invigorates the Soul*, puts it, "[P]lay seems to
be one of the most advanced methods nature has invented to allow
a complex brain to invent itself."[7] Because play is fundamentally a
nonessential activity permitting plenty of room for trial and error,
it permits the brain to create, test, and organize new neural connections to see what works and what does not, making play an essential
factor in long-term brain growth, development, and adaptability.

Despite our adult perception that we gave up playing years ago,
it turns out that we all have a drive to play throughout our life span,
even when we are working right up to the edge of our capacity.
In fact, if we deny ourselves the opportunity to play over the long

---

[7]   Stuart Brown and Christopher Vaughan, *Play: How It Shapes the Brain,
Opens the Imagination, and Invigorates the Soul* (Washington, DC:
National Geographic Books, 2010).

haul, we can experience a discernable increase in negativity and an inability to experience pleasure or creative impulses.

Given the benefits of play to continued brain health and overall well-being, I find it useful to help my clients rediscover their own personal brand of play using Dr. Brown's "play personalities." Before I delve into these, let's consider his definition of play. He sees it as a state of mind more than a specific activity—an absorbing and essentially purposeful endeavor that has the dual effect of causing pleasure and also suspending a sense of time and self-consciousness. It is engagement done for enjoyment's sake, even if there are practical rewards associated with it.

According to Dr. Brown's extensive research, there are the eight play personalities, and an individual can fit into several of these categories:

- The "Joker" loves to joke around and play practical jokes on others. Their brand of play revolves around some form of nonsense or silliness.
- The "Kinesthete" must engage in physical movement and is happiest in activities that push their bodies such as dancing, running, or skiing. They often need to move to think.
- The "Explorer" has a hankering to explore new places and experiences and delights in activities such as hiking, travel, and experiencing new foods and cultures. They might also explore emotionally—through music, poetry, or relationships—or mentally, through learning or research.
- The "Competitor" is compelled to compete with others and seeks out activities such as sports, games, and challenges. They relish games, keeping score, and winning.

- The "Director" can't help but plan and organize activities, execute strategies, and catalyze group experiences. They are the party throwers and travel or event planners who adore both putting the plan together and then watching others enjoy it.
- The "Collector" loves to cull the best array of items, such as stamps, coins, or figurines, or a specific set of experiences, such as reaching the highest point of every US state.
- The "Artist/Creator" heeds the siren of creative self-expression and is drawn to activities such as painting, drawing, and writing. They derive joy in making entirely new things or repairing or refurbishing items into something beautiful or functional.
- The "Storyteller" has a passion for telling stories, engaging the imagination, and experiencing the drama of existence through the lens of story. They might be authors, screenwriters, or oral storytellers but equally love to consume stories that others tell through reading, watching movies, or seeing live performances.

As our clients share stories about their most engaging and enjoyable experiences, whether in professional or personal spaces, their specific play personalities emerge before our eyes. Once we help them name these treasured engagements as a form of play, their minds open up to new realms of possibility for meaningful enjoyment. And they often realize they have been starved for the rejuvenation provided by conscious play.

If we stop playing, science tells us we share a common fate—our behaviors become fixed, we lose our curiosity, and our interest in new and different experiences declines. In short, we find fewer and fewer ways to take pleasure from the world around us. For our clients, unlocking their often-starved play personalities creates a spark of energy and enthusiasm for what lies ahead. It is an aspect of their identity that easily comes back to life once identified.

One of my favorite memories of this moment occurred when Harvey, a fairly cranky fund manager from New York, shared his fascination with discovering old bars in any city he visited. He would actively seek out the oldest neighborhood watering hole he could find with the intention of pulling up a barstool and engaging the bartender in a discussion about the establishment's origin story and often colorful path of survival. As he described this quirky habit of his, his entire posture changed. He became animated. He smiled. And his face was full of amusement and pleasure as he recalled the minutest details of his adventures. Here was Harvey, the serious, no-frills deal businessman, secretly playing at his own game outside his usual conference room habitat. It was clear to me that he was a natural storyteller and collector—that these forms of engagement were pure play to him.

I asked Harvey, "What if, just for fun, you actually mapped out the oldest bars in America and then visited each one with a plan to profile it?" He leaned in with a focused enthusiasm. "You could reach out in advance, arrange for the right people to be there, and interview them to get the history of the bar and its role in shaping the surrounding community. This could be a great way to capture and preserve these stories—maybe as a series of articles at first, but ultimately a book. What do you think?" Suffice it to say that Harvey was off and running. The idea seized him almost instantly, and it became an anchor of his plans for the future, encompassing as it did his love of history, travel, storytelling, and curating this unique collection of places in America.

A Formula for Resilience

Setbacks, adversity, crisis. This unwanted trio is as certain as death and taxes. By the time retirement is looming, our clients have navigated them all at various points in their lives and careers, but rarely can they name their formula for doing so. And yet, when prompted to tell their stories, it becomes obvious that they have a method for gaining their bearings, assessing the scope of the situation, and then moving forward, often capitalizing on what appeared to be a catastrophic undoing.

A common theme we see is the ability to find a pathway to concrete action. Whether they are conscious of it or not, our clients seem to have a cache of strategies that permit them to face an unwanted calamity and do whatever they can to achieve victory, even if that simply means accepting a situation they cannot change and capitalizing on new angles of opportunity.

For example, a number of our clients have faced life-threatening illnesses during the spans of their demanding careers, and their stories are always inspiring. These distressing circumstances seemingly come out of the blue and present a potentially life-altering threat that, even if surmounted, sidetracks professional progress in one way or another. While retirement is not, on its face, in the same category as a serious illness, it can create similar sensations of fear, dread, and impending loss. Recognizing that you have triumphed over adversity before and you have a proven method for doing so can be a valuable exercise.

When Jennifer approached us to work with her about the idea of retiring, she was still sorting out the timing. As a successful mergers and acquisitions lawyer, she was still plenty busy. Lately, however, she had been feeling as if she'd lost her edge. She was questioning whether the time had come to move on from the practice of law, but like many in her position, the lack of a game plan had left her feeling oddly indecisive. She suddenly found herself struggling to identify a target date for her retirement, which, in turn, made it nearly impossible to begin thinking about what might come next. This chicken-and-egg conundrum privately filled her with embarrassment and confusion.

During our morning session together, we asked Jennifer to tell us about a setback or crisis she had faced in her life. She unfolded a defining story about her unexpected colon cancer diagnosis at age forty-three. Her disease was on an aggressive course, and she'd been told that she only had a 26 percent chance of surviving another year. Jennifer was in the prime of her life and career at the time, having made partner at a very prestigious Wall Street firm only six years earlier. Her children were relatively young, and she deeply cared about her husband. For Jennifer, it was a perfect storm: an unexpected crisis she could not control, and even if she survived, it risked sidelining all she had worked for professionally. As she relayed those painful early days of her diagnosis, we asked her, "Tell us what you did to move yourself forward—what first steps did you take?"

Being a person who tends to lead with her intellect, Jennifer explained that she first sought to become educated about her disease. She consulted credible studies and multiple doctors to ground herself in knowledge so she could operate from a position of greater competence. "I needed to understand the treatments that were out there but also how and why they worked," she elaborated. And although she felt under pressure to begin treatment, she made the time to solicit a range of professional opinions regarding both the prognosis and the course of treatment.

Recognizing that she would need support in managing her tendency to be pessimistic, she engaged (for the first time in her life) a therapist. She discovered that optimism has more to do with feeling empowered in a situation than it does with expecting it to turn out "just fine," which is an insight she carries with her to this day. Jennifer is not someone who readily shares her personal challenges in the work setting, yet she realized she would need to confide in a close circle of trusted colleagues. Not only would they cover for her when she was physically down, but they'd also stand as sources of encouragement that she could emerge victorious with her professional world intact. These work relationships are now deep and enduring friendships.

As Jennifer described her combined strategies of educating herself, consulting experts, and seeking support, she could readily see how she was able to get into action and ultimately prevail over an obstacle that had initially paralyzed her. Having come out the other side, Jennifer also observed that she was stronger for the whole experience—more optimistic than pessimistic and more confident in her ability to deal with crisis and adversity. She added that she had since been able to guide several other individuals facing a similar situation, providing both resources and encouragement. For Jennifer, these opportunities have proven to be extremely rewarding. What's more, in the course of fighting her medical battle, which she ultimately won, she and her spouse strengthened their partnership enormously.

Jennifer's story highlights a few important points. First, part of our enduring self includes our own unique formula for resilience. As we have confronted prior episodes of adversity, we can see that we have a reserve of effective strategies for getting into action and maintaining momentum, even when it takes the sheer force of will to carry on. Whether professional or personal, we have navigated plenty of obstacles along the way, and yet here we are. Retirement— at worst, unwanted, and at best, unsettling—will be just another challenge in a long line of many. And finally, we can see that the adversity we have faced en route has actually made us stronger, better, more aware of our abilities, and more understanding of the struggles faced by others. Retirement presents a new opportunity to deploy our tried-and-true methods for facing challenges and, consequently, expand and deepen these aspects of ourselves.

Chapter Summary

Because it is easy to conflate who we are with what we do for a living, it is useful to consider what humanistic psychologists can tell us about our self-concept, its formation, and its component parts.

According to Carl Rogers, our self-concept is composed of our self-image (how we see ourselves), our self-esteem (how we feel about ourselves), and our self-ideal (the version of ourselves we'd most like to be). Our professional lives have typically provided strong content in shaping these components.

Our self-concept has existential or enduring aspects as well as categorical or role-based aspects. As we consider moving beyond our professional roles, it is helpful to connect with the parts of our identity that will continue on into the future.

In examining the existential facets of identity, it is possible to uncover themes relating to purpose, process, and aspiration. Often, these elements of our identity can be traced back to our earlier experiences and can be leveraged to shape our future but yet unknown endeavors.

While working professionals rarely admit to wanting or needing to play, science tells us that play is instrumental in shaping continued brain growth and development. Dr. Stuart Brown's "play personalities" offer a window into how adults play, even when that play is masked by productivity. This component of identity can shine a light on future areas of engagement.

An impending retirement can generate the same concerns we have when confronted with adversity in life. Examining an individual's unique approach to navigating adversity and to building resilience offers insight into methods that might be helpful as they construct a path through retirement and into a new chapter.

chapter six

SHAPING THE FUTURE OF YOU

When I let go of what I am, I become what I might be.
~ Lao Tzu, philosopher

When Roles Collide

This was a peak moment. It was a blustery fall day in 2003. I was freshly back from maternity leave and now leading one of the largest international financing deals of the era. Sheathed in my navy-blue Burberry suit, I was perched at the head of an enormous table in a packed conference room in an elite law firm. My audience was an assemblage of the most important lawyers involved in the matter at hand, the matter I was holding forth about. Then the commotion started. It was all going on two feet behind me.

About an hour earlier, I had finally seized a break in the action to address a rather urgent need to commune with my breast pump. Now, unbeknownst to me, the wholesome yield was ominously spreading across the conference room credenza into an enormous puddle. With each passing moment, its borders expanded. My two junior associates, registering the unthinkable, ran over with wads of napkins to staunch the expanding lake. There they were, frantically mopping up my breast milk, which had somehow escaped its innocuous-looking carrier and resolutely claimed most of the surrounding surface area. The crowning insult was its visible saturation of one fellow's *very* expensive leather briefcase.

"Did somebody spill creamer?" he intoned, somewhat frantically. "What is this? Where's it coming from?" *Compartmentalize or die*, whispered my inner guardian angel. So I kept right on working throughout the whole unseemly ordeal. At no point did I claim responsibility for this horror. There was just no acceptable explanation. *Trust me, you don't actually want to know what this is*, I imagined telling this gentleman and the roomful of male lawyers assembled to do business.

Hopefully, he never figured out the source of that mystery leak. Had he realized it, he would have thrown his briefcase out the window and run out of the building. It would have just been too much. This was the early 2000s, after all, and things like breast pumps and breast milk were to be neither seen nor heard.

This collision of my all-important roles of mother and lawyer was a defining moment. The inner conversation that echoes through all the years since went down like this: *I just managed to soak someone's luxurious leather briefcase in my breast milk while I'm simultaneously negotiating a $1.2 billion deal. That's seems oddly incongruous. I wonder what the universe is trying to tell me. If this is a sign from above, then someone has a wicked sense of humor.*

At this moment, I began to understand that I could not harmonize these two aspects of my life. I knew I had to let my career go, but leaving was bittersweet. At my ensuing farewell party, the managing partner of my office said the usual kind words about my tenure and contributions to the firm and my colleagues. Though I had never shown the slightest weakness at the firm before then, I spontaneously burst into tears. It hit me like a ton of bricks that I was leaving a place that felt like family to me. It was the right thing for me to do, but no less sad for being right.

And here is where the connection between roles and identity is visible. As identified as I was with being a lawyer at my firm, once I had children, I became just as identified with being a mother. My law career had assumed galactic importance in my life, and yet there were new aspects of my identity that clamored to be heard. When I look back on it, I have to wonder: Who was that woman sitting in that conference room trying to pump her breast milk, check all the mommy boxes, and simultaneously run a huge, international deal? It seems almost incomprehensible to me that I thought I could conquer both worlds—and shine in both roles with an A-plus—at once.

The breast milk fandango was the moment I realized, *What I'm trying to do is impractical—at least for me.* On reflection, it was ludicrously funny, but it also stopped me short. There was no denying it: my roles as successful deal lawyer and fully involved mother were not happy bedfellows; one of them would have to go—and it was obvious which one.

I share this somewhat dismaying story as a bit of levity and as a lens into how much our roles influence our sense of who we are and who we think we should be. Even when it's your own choice to abandon a role, it can feel absolutely distressing to let it go. While I did make the decision to leave my career of my own volition, in terms of my identity, it felt like I had lopped off an arm. I knew it was not feasible for me to continue in this career and also be the mother I wanted to be. And yet redeeming my professional self was still something I had to work out after the fact. I had to construct a new professional persona for myself that provided the same validation and psychological reward loops being a lawyer had provided. Even though I perceived myself to have many different interests and ideas for engagement, I still found the loss of my lawyer role daunting and complicated. Eventually, I realized I needed to reconstruct the part of my identity that used my talents and abilities beyond nurturing my kids and managing my home. I was not fully satisfied by the roles of mom and household boss. Though I had a big investment in both, they didn't use all the parts of me that I value.

My early-career departure for full-time motherhood shares a theme with my clients who are opting into retirement, particularly before the required age. For example, culturally, it might be the right thing to do to make room for younger lawyers. But having a good reason to go does not equate with being ready to go. And this confusion is usually, in part, about the impending loss of a key aspect of one's categorical identity.

The Importance of the Categorical Identity

While our categorial identities are not, fundamentally, who we are, they represent an important aspect of how we see ourselves. As the above story demonstrates, part of the identity we construct is built on the various associations we have with others and the myriad roles we play in our lives. Social identity theory, introduced by Henri Tajfel and his associates in the late 1970s, describes how a person's self-concept is shaped by their sense of belonging to particular social groups. Sports teams, religions, nationalities, careers, racial and ethnic groups, and gender are a few examples. Social identities matter most when we place a high value on belonging to a certain group and develop deep emotional connections accordingly, as in, "I am a partner at such-and-such elite firm." Claiming that role and being a part of that group increases self-esteem, and being cast out of that group can send a person's self-esteem into free fall.

The importance of roles to our self-concept does not stop with mere emotional connection and belonging. Our own assessment of how we show up in critical roles has a significant impact on our overall positive self-regard, which can also have an outsize impact on everything from motivation and discipline to behavior and overall psychological state. In 1977, psychologist Albert Bandura coined the term "self-efficacy," referring to a person's belief in their ability to successfully execute on a course of action in a particular set of circumstances. These cognitive self-evaluations affect all manner of human behavior, including the goals for which people strive, the amount of energy expended toward goal achievement, and the likelihood of attaining particular levels of behavioral performance. When we have an overall strong sense of self-efficacy, measured in part by how we think we show up in the important roles we play, we are more likely to face a new challenge with greater commitment, enjoyment, and resilience. Conversely, if our feeling of self-efficacy is weaker, that same challenge can create behaviors like avoidance and denial, resulting in a failure to meet a new challenge, or even to try.

This helps explain why I clung to my relationship to Milbank and to my role as a lawyer when I introduced myself, even months after I had left Washington, DC and moved to a city where no one had ever heard of that law firm. In my mind, albeit unconsciously, it remained an important factor of my worth and sense of belonging. Without it, I was unsure of how I could demonstrate my competence and abilities to those I met. The loss of the role of lawyer and my community at work threatened to upend my hard-won self-efficacy, and I could literally feel my once robust self-confidence ebbing away.

Reconciling Roles

Because retirement, at its heart, spells the loss of major professional roles and categories of belonging, we spend time with our clients digging into their own inventory of roles and assessments of their self-efficacy in those roles. The exercise is always revealing.

We ask our clients, "We know you are a *lawyer*, of course, but what are the other hats you wear in your professional life?" For most, there are seven to ten sub-roles that make up the overarching legal career. For example, one might break their professional role of "lawyer" into the following: partner, adviser, practice group leader, mentor, business developer, and technical expert. When asked to rate their perception of their performance in all these roles, they typically rate themselves very highly. They acknowledge that they perform well, and they are proud of what they do in those roles. For obvious reasons, these roles provide strong feedback loops that enhance positive self-efficacy and overall self-regard.

When we get into their personal lives, the picture sometimes changes. To begin with, fewer roles obtain, and they often do not allow themselves the high ratings of the professional realm. This is commonly because the hard-driving individual has been time starved and, in their estimation, has not invested enough of themselves in these roles to deserve a top rating.

We next ask them to imagine removing the numerous professional roles for which the scores are highest. Almost instantly, a light bulb goes on, and they can see that the sudden loss of their professional roles could be problematic indeed. Their self-esteem stands to be diminished because every place they feel that they shine suddenly disappears. Without a plan to build new replacement roles, it's a recipe for a spiral into depression and low self-esteem. Few can create from that place. Few can pursue dreams from that place. Few can see possibility from that place.

Revisiting our session with Peggy Davenport, she recalls the exercise on roles and what she found especially helpful:

> You had me list my identities. So I say, mother, wife, sister, friend—and I am done with my personal life. Then I move over to my work: negotiator, mentor, strategist, manager, you know, blah, blah, executive, and I rattle off all my professional identities, and then I'm done. And you're looking at me again, as if to ask, "Nothing else?" I'm like, "No, no, we're done here." And you're like, "I'll give you a little hint: marathon." And I go, "Oh yeah, I'm a runner. But that's not my identity." Your next prompt has to do with plane tickets. I say, "Oh yeah, I travel all over the place, but I'm not a traveler." I had this all neatly organized in my brain—there's work and

there's life, and life is just about these relationships. There wasn't a single hobby on my list.

Eventually, I had to rank myself according to my listed identities. What I took away from the exercise is that when you remove this work piece and all these things where you're giving yourself an eight to ten, you're kind of in trouble. Because unless you have phenomenal familial relations and friendships that are going to keep your score up, you're going down once you take the work out.

What we explain to people is that it's wonderful they found a career and devised all these ways to enrich others and themselves by making valuable contributions. It's okay that these things are coming to some form of closure because it means they have a huge and exciting opportunity to look to the future for fresh ways to engage that probably have more to do with their wisdom than with their ability to work hard and earn money. The quest to attach new meaning to their lives can be transcendent. But, as we tell them, "Don't try to do it from a place where you have chopped yourself off at the knees."

Beware the "End of History" Illusion

As we attempt to think forward about ourselves, it is important to be aware of a mental deception that can get in our way: namely, that we tend to think of ourselves right now as the full and final expression of who we will ever be. Of course, when we reflect back on our younger selves, they are clearly considerably different. Hindsight is twenty-twenty. We are aware, in retrospect, of how much our personality traits and preferences have transformed from one life stage to another. Yet when we gaze ahead, curiously, we anticipate a continuation of who we are at this moment. A team of psychologists advanced these findings in 2013, coining the phrase the "end of history illusion," whereby people "underestimate how much they will change in the future."[8] What the researchers were seeing in individuals spanning ages from eighteen to sixty-eight was the "illusion" of having become at present the person they will now forever be. The risk associated with dialing down our expectation of personal evolution lies in designing plans for our future selves based on current preferences we will surely outgrow.

One of the key authors of this study, Harvard professor and happiness expert Daniel Gilbert, presented a wildly popular TED Talk underscoring this tendency of people to underestimate how much they will change in the future. This trick of the mind, shown to be universal across ages, cultures, and backgrounds, can lead people to make decisions based on their current preferences and goals, rather than considering how these might change in the future. He offered relatable examples. I especially chuckled at this one: "Middle-aged people rush to divorce people whom as young adults they rushed to marry." But his more serious question is this: "Why do we make decisions that our future selves so often regret?" The simple answer is that we all mistakenly believe our personal history has reached its ultimate destination—at whatever moment we happen to be. And the fundamental reason for this is the difficulty we tend to have imagining our future selves compared to the relative ease of remembering who we have been and how we got there.

But, importantly, research confirms that we remain works in progress over the entire course of our lives. Our skills, tastes, and personality markers continue to morph over time, and the exercise of imagining and shaping those changes is crucial for anyone envisioning life after they retire, where we often have no script at all. Otherwise, we risk making decisions and choices that fit our

---

[8]   Quoidbach, Jordi, Daniel T. Gilbert, and Timothy D. Wilson. "The End of History Illusion." *Science* 339, no. 6115 (January 4, 2013): 96–98. https://doi.org/10.1126/science.1229294.

narratives in middle adulthood, missing the mark on who we are on our way to becoming. Imagination, then, is an important but often dormant aptitude to nurture ahead of retirement.

Flexing the Imagination Muscle

How do you move toward the evolving version of yourself if you struggle to imagine it? As a start, you might begin by recognizing the differences between who you were in the past and who you are at present. It follows that where you are right now is not your final destiny. The future you is coming, and that person most probably will not want to do the same things "current" you enjoys. But what might those new things be? To help people past that blind spot, we stimulate their imaginations to unpeel the web of goals and visions for the self they seek to become.

Most people in intense service professions are out of practice when it comes to using their imaginations. Because they have so much content coming at them, they are reacting, not imagining or creating. Mental exploration, open space, what if?—no one has time for that. Planning for the case or task at hand consumes their bandwidth. And yet. "Dreaming, after all, is a form of planning," Gloria Steinem astutely observed. One of the planning capacities we try to reawaken is the imagination, especially as it relates to an evolving and future identity.

Of course, the brain can only handle so much future projection. Most people cannot picture forever. Forever is too vast. We spare them the fog of answering free-floating questions such as, "What do you want to do with the rest of your life?" An interval like the next ten years offers a more manageable way for the mind to try out new ideas. Just as the studies surrounding the end of history illusion study were pinned to a specific time frame, we ask our participants to pretend they're at the end of the coming decade. The time-skipping prompt goes something like this: "What will you have accomplished in ten years that will move you to look back on and say, 'That was an incredible decade'?" We ask them to think about how they have affected the people in their lives over this decade. "Imagine you're being celebrated ten years from now," we begin the prompt. "It's a big birthday, and you're surrounded by friends, family, and colleagues. What are the things you hope to hear from this array of people who have been in your midst?"

The big takeaway is that it's never about money or accolades. Rather, the attainments we hear that will make respondents proud are always about being there for others; making a difference; showing kindness; being a good friend, parent, or spouse. Their current definitions of success, often heavily defined by career matters, are revealed as a slender hook on which to hang their future hopes and dreams. They can see that nobody's going to toast them for their bank account or for the big case they won. What's going to matter is that they're healthy and making a difference to the people in their world. Most arrive at this realization and say, "Well, of course that's true, but I never had time to think about it." Now they can see that the success box, which is so important to their current self, is checked. *Time to move off the mountain and tune my mind to different aspirations.*

Exploring what high-powered people wish to feel more of in the coming decade is also revealing. When we put this query to participants, variations on the theme of "peaceful" often arise. As in, "I want everything to calm down around me so I can feel at peace," or "I want to feel serene." The craving for tranquility comes across loud and clear from people who have been subjected to high-stress jobs for many years. Understandably so, given the punishing workweeks they have endured. And in the case of lawyers, there's all too often the added pressure of winning court cases or closing huge deals, especially under the glare of the national or international news media. It can feel nearly impossible to imagine a life of relevance and engagement without the all-consuming intensity and pressure that have so far defined their experiences. More on this point in chapter 7.

Embracing New Mindsets

This brings me to the all-important topic of mindsets. To survive and thrive in our post-career lives, we need to break free of old mental enclosures, often those that have been key to our professional achievements. For example, as I noted in chapter 4, Erikson's psychosocial stages of development posit that we have a drive during middle adulthood to test and measure ourselves against our highest potential. This naturally sets up a mindset of measuring our value and purpose through the lens of external success factors, such as income, accolades, promotions, and power. The end of a career naturally presents the potential for these particular feedback loops to diminish or end altogether—a scary prospect for a mind accustomed to these sources of validation. The question looms: *How do I take success further?*

And what about that sense of mastery and competence that every professional possesses after years at their chosen avocation? By the time retirement is upon us, we are proven authorities in our fields, and we enjoy the expert mindset, providing as it does the security and comfort of being the one with the answers. The idea of trying new things we need time to master feels almost embarrassing, like a display of bad manners.

But perhaps the most powerful mindset undergirding a professional's way of thinking is the long-standing pattern of reacting to the nonstop content coming at them. This is the province of most intense professionals: content, problems, crises, and projects fly at them relentlessly like tennis balls from a practice machine, and the skill of reacting with speed and precision is the resulting superpower. The "reactor" mindset is as embedded as DNA, but the "creator" mindset? Not so much.

Part of loosening the grip of existing mindsets is asking questions like "What are your new measures going to be?" and "How are you going to check in with yourself during the coming decade to confirm you are pleased with the direction you're moving in?" As we point out, it won't be because you hit your sales targets, billed more hours, or received a bigger bonus. Without the habitual metrics and comparisons, it is important to understand how you will define progress and chart it for yourself. It's at this juncture that the end of history illusion, discussed earlier, is especially instructive. We use it as a caveat against importing potentially obsolete mindsets into the imagined decade ahead when the occasion of retirement affords a clean break.

Let's take a closer look at evolving from the "success" mindset to that of usefulness or contribution. For many who have been recognized as the best in their fields, this is a challenging shift. But it seems to be a standard occupational hazard. Most elite, professional settings are structured as competitive environments where their inhabitants are measured against and compared to their peers. They're always watching for someone to overtake them. An invisible scorecard hovers menacingly overhead, flashing every win and loss for others to evaluate. *Am I good enough this month? This year?* The extent of one's success hangs in the balance at all times for external forces to decide. Whatever the most recent success was, it must be bested, or else the trend line is negative. There is no winning that game. The minute victory is in hand is the minute you start over. It can be a very demoralizing way of navigating life.

The catch with this mindset of success and its close pal, competition, is that one can never finally say, "I've done it. I'm successful." As one highly accomplished rock star reflected, "Intense work environments have a way of making very successful people feel very unsuccessful."

Retirement offers a chance to drop the mindset of success and competition. What a relief! In the future, yours is the only opinion that really matters. When your own sense of usefulness and contribution becomes the focus of your progress, you can enjoy the peace and serenity that comes with setting the metrics and keeping your own score. Finally, you can lay down the rules of the professional jungle. But first, you must acknowledge they have been governing your behavior for a very long time.

The mindset of "expert," connoting as it does mastery and competence, can also limit obvious pathways for growth and expansion. It is not unusual for our clients to lament that they have no creative life. Some of their stories map the perimeters of yearning and regret. Musicians, artists, writers, actors, dancers—these are but five of the would-be creative callings that often get subordinated to a practical career choice like law or accounting. In the glare of honesty, the soon-to-retire professional might express a wistfulness, or even a still-burning desire, to give their dormant talent a whirl. Yet some remain too easily intimidated after decades of muzzled expression and loathe the idea of being a novice. Even—or especially—having reached the apex of their profession, they feel ill-equipped to pursue their dream, focused as they are on feeling competent in all they do.

The careworn immediately put their ideas through the performance machine. *Will I succeed? Will the world applaud me for this? If not, why bother?* For those individuals who are slow to appreciate the fruitless logic they're cultivating, we try to underscore that any engagement they take on must be for their love of its potential, not for the love of others' approval.

In particular, writing leaves its share of openings for anxious questers. Many of the professionals we coach possess a secret dream of becoming writers. But the notion can get garbled into a preoccupation with being published. The encouragement we supply accentuates the positive rewards of the creative process while softening the drumbeat of fancied glory. If you love the process of synthesizing ideas, researching, and writing, and that's enough, the publishing part will probably take care of itself. But if you need a guarantee at the front end that your literary chops will be instantly hailed by the world, then you've put yourself back in a transactional mode where it's all about third-party approval and success, another unwinnable game.

The answer, then, is not to bring the mindset of expert into these new endeavors but rather, that of a student. While it has been a long time since most of our participants have been apprentices, the concept is nevertheless familiar and approachable. Anyone who has climbed to the top of an intense profession first summited an academic mountain. This reframe is a reminder that their current mastery was born out of committed study and practice. Now, there is an accessible way to engage with a new, if intimidating, endeavor.

Embracing the mindset of a student does not mean following every prospect. We warn our participants to stay aware of their ingrained "reactor" mindset, thinking carefully about the invitations they accept in this postcareer chapter. Being good at something, on its own, is not a sufficient reason to do it. Professionals are so habituated to saying, "Yes, of course." Their orientation is never "What do I want?" It's always "What is being asked of me?" This contingent way of thinking, whether conscious or not, is simply the requisite mindset to excel as a service provider or executive. Reacting to the needs and problems of others often means we are not the drivers of what instigates the action we take. While many have been creative in how they solved problems, they have still been living inside the box of the problem that someone else gave them.

The key advice we provide our clients is "You want to move from reactor to creator." Inherent in this paradigm shift is a call for pulse-taking. Is the idea feeling expansive and on purpose for you? Is it full of rich, juicy stuff? Or is it more like a concession to your proven strengths? *I know I'll get an A if I do it, but I'm not very excited by it.* For individuals who are habituated to reacting and saying yes, it's easy to fall prey to the trap of *Well, of course I should do it because it showed up, and I'm good at it.* But we remind them that the days of compulsory reacting are largely behind them, and now the joys of choosing what they want to do, when they want to do it, and who they do it with belong to them. All of which is at the heart of imagining and creating the possible selves that inhabit a rich and energizing future.

Howard Marks, Meet Your Possible Self

Our two days with soon-to-be former lawyer Howard Marks, whom we met in chapter 4, gave us a glimmer of this push-pull with his possible self. Like most lawyers seeking their next stage of engagement, Howard had achieved everything he had hoped for in his practice of law and wanted a fresh challenge. But having done one thing for decades, he simply could not imagine what else to do. As with most of our participants, there was a fear factor. And a certain pull of inertia. But in parallel with those dynamics, he wanted a genuine and exciting pathway for the future. With his goal states triggered, Howard appeared ready to entertain a huge pivot. Often, it is just what we are looking for: the sometimes nonobvious "possible self."

Possible selves theory, developed by Canadian psychologist Hazel Markus and her colleagues, posits that an individual's sense of self is, in part, based on the possible selves they imagine. These possible selves can be either ideal selves, which represent the person's hopes and aspirations for the future, or feared selves, which represent the person's fears and anxieties about the future. For Markus et al., in step with Albert Bandura's self-efficacy concept, the way individuals think about and pursue their possible selves can have a significant impact on their motivation, behavior, and well-being. Individuals who have clear and positive visions of their ideal selves tend to be more motivated, engaged, and resilient while those who are preoccupied with their feared selves may be more anxious, avoidant, and disengaged. This work has huge implications for how professionals like Howard think about themselves as they contemplate retiring.

Howard arrived at eight-thirty a.m. on the dot. Before we broke for lunch, David and I had absorbed the basic grammar of his identity and story, who he was authentically, and what he really loved about his career. For us, these foundational hours afford deep learning. We listen for clues about other parts of people's lives that have probably gone a bit dormant because of the demands of their work. It's not unusual for lawyers to put 80 percent of their waking hours, if not more, into the profession. Small wonder many lose touch with the parts of themselves that made them feel fully alive as younger men or women. Getting back to that creative self can be tough. Years of advancing on one path has usually left them with tunnel vision. Part of our process is about reopening that horizon: what we call "shaking the snow globe." Individuals who come for coaching often hear us say, "We're going to stir up a lot of material. We see a fixed sense of who you are. Now let's turn all that settled thinking upside down and see what looks possible again."

One of the first things that swirled up with Howard is that, fundamentally, he's a people person. All his most satisfying experiences involved engagement and collaboration with others. It's perhaps not the first assumption one might make about a corporate lawyer. But it was true for him.

We heard it in the way he talked about the possibility of teaching, which seemed like a reasonable and accessible idea. Having conducted his share of seminars as a guest lecturer at a prestigious university, he had considered retiring into the classroom as an obvious progression. And he ascribed one of his strengths as a corporate lawyer to his knack for focusing on the overall objectives of his transactions, as opposed to the meaningless technical points that some lawyers insist on winning. That lesson had been catechized by his mentor, whom he still remembers saying, "I never want you to waste time negotiating silly issues that do not affect the client's goals. I want you to focus on what the client is trying to achieve on a business level and pick your battles accordingly." Howard carried this discipline over to the students he was invited to instruct.

> I would work up complex case studies and really drive home the connections between the legal issues and the business objectives, but over time, I began to feel as if my engagement and commitment weren't

really being matched by the students themselves. It's the dynamic exchanges that really excite me.

The reciprocation he'd hoped for turned out to be sorely lacking. These scant rewards for long hours of solitary prep dampened his enthusiasm for academia. "There is an element of isolation to teaching, which is something I want to get away from," Howard told us. His love of creating in a group context surfaced ever more distinctly in the explorations we conducted with him. Looking back, he now muses:

> Our session was very helpful because we started by zooming out above the details to focus on the big picture first. Not a lot of tactics, at first, but more generally, *What do I want?* My best times at the firm were in management roles working with an incredibly skilled, smart, capable group of people on a shared goal—improvising and iterating along the way.

As our facilitation progressed, we started noticing another theme. Howard delves deeply into any topic he finds intriguing. Examples abounded with each vignette he relayed. But without realizing it, Howard was telling us story after story about his hobby as a jazz pianist. It's the one pursuit he has had a love affair with ever since he was a small boy. He was not only talented as a player but extremely knowledgeable as a historian. He had even composed music and helped organize jam sessions with other jazz musicians. What popped for both David and me when we shared notes about the exchange was Howard's encyclopedic knowledge of all aspects of jazz—not just playing the music. Duly noted.

We further observed that Howard had a strong desire to continue contributing in a way that felt like he was capitalizing on his wisdom and knowledge. Our task was to help him do just that.

Because one of the goals of our two-day sessions is to generate new ideas, sometimes what bobs up feels pretty crazy and out there. But we treat it all like brainstorming, and nothing is off limits. The ethos is "Throw it all at the wall." We are not allowed to judge ideas until we produce lots of them. Only then can the editing begin.

At one point in our explorations, David and I asked Howard how he might feel about engaging with jazz in a more focused way. His answer came with a qualifier. "Well," he explained, "playing the piano isn't enough. That's not going to keep me fulfilled by itself. . . . Of course, I like it, and I'll do it, but it's not going to create a sense of purpose in my life."

That's when it hit us. Howard has a uniquely honed expertise about jazz music. His knowledge is broad and goes deep. He knows *everything* about this topic. And Howard is a great conversationalist who loves the give-and-take of energized dialogue.

"What if you started a podcast about jazz music?" I ventured as we braced for the telltale response.

Howard just lit up. "Oh my gosh, what a good idea!"

Next, we jumped into the details. "It could be an interview format, and you could bring on people from all over the jazz world— owners of jazz clubs, makers of instruments, historical figures in jazz, teachers, you name it." Howard's eyes widened even more with interest. And yet.

Howard's excitement collided with his equally potent expert mindset. Like many of our clients, he echoed the "Yes, but" refrain we've so often heard at a certain point in a conversation. Resistance reared its frightened head. "Oh, I love that idea, but I have no idea how to do it," he protested, adding,

> I don't see what qualifies me to do it. I have no idea how to create a podcast. I'm not good at that kind thing. I mean, I would love to have those conversations, but how do you do a podcast? And if I figured it out, who would listen to it?

If the prospect of a life after law generally filled him with angst, the notion of a future possible self as a podcaster specifically triggered his dread.

And yet, we could see the idea intrigued him. We just had to convince him not to lawyer the idea to death. We asked him, for now, to drop his concerns about whether he would succeed and how he would acquire the skills. Instead, we asked him who he knew in his circle who might be able to help him explore this idea. Howard recalls his first tentative steps.

> I've had a long friendship with another jazz musician. Whenever we spend time together, we end up talking for hours about jazz. He had appeared on a few podcasts, so I asked him if he could put me on touch with one of them. He was thrilled to help.

Going further with this idea, Howard asked his friend if he could interview him for the first episode of his own podcast—just to give it a try and see how it felt. "Worst case, I'll delete the thing and pretend it never happened." The seed we had planted was starting to germinate.

> Looking back, beyond the question of how to do a podcast, my hesitation was really the fear of rejection. I really prize the feeling of competence, so it was uncomfortable for me to reach out like this in an area where I don't yet feel masterful. But I did have to ask, *What's the harm if someone says no?* It's not like my livelihood is dependent on this working. There's literally nothing riding on it but my own ego. This is really no meaningful risk associated with failure here.

Howard would follow our advice to experiment with something unfamiliar yet of deep resonance and to see where it might lead him. Before long, Howard had secured a URL. He figured out how to set up his tech rig. He recorded his first two episodes. We coached him about basic marketing outreach, from LinkedIn to his own website, and we too shared his debut podcasts with our audience.

He constantly networked—though seldom would he bring up his podcast concept in those early days. Nonetheless, the folks he reached out to peopled his dream list of invitees, just as we had suggested. In time, he began generating his own strong word of mouth. Over the next two years, he implemented our proposed plan step by step. Howard's outreach landed him decisive breakthroughs along the way, and his list of willing guests began to grow.

As the podcast continued to gain traction, Howard literally put his money where his mouth was. He outfitted his house with a mini–recording studio replete with soundproof padding, quality headphones and microphones, and podcast editing software, among other accoutrements. Although interviewing people online was a departure from anything he'd done before, much of his preproduction work involved skills he had honed over his long career. He conducted deep research about his upcoming guests and prepared open-ended and intriguing questions that would provide the opportunity for Howard and his guests to improvise and engage in wide-ranging conversations. Before long, Howard's identity began to expand to include his love of jazz, as did his community.

A second tier of Howard's jazz-themed retirement saw him join a local jazz band, which eventually booked gigs and hooked into the house concert community. This calling sends Howard on the road as often as twice a month, depending on where his band is playing.

Beyond podcasting and jam sessions, the third tier of Howard's retirement has enabled him to pour time and energy into elevating younger musicians and energizing jazz festivals that create opportunities for the public and musicians alike to deepen their relationship with music. Howard has firmly established his place at the local jazz scene, and he is making unique and lasting contributions to this rich world.

Howard's evolution into a multifaceted relationship with music didn't happen overnight. Instead, he had to gradually step out of his comfort zone one rung at a time, dropping his concerns about things like success and mastery. Trying on this "possible self" was mission critical for him, and it took some courage—and *will*, in the beginning.

> My discomfort in trying something new was something that I had to get past, and it was really helpful to talk about it during our session. Since doing the podcast and playing live in more and more situations, I've developed momentum and so much more confidence. My comfort zone has expanded enormously.

Today, Howard's podcast is north of sixty episodes and counting. Howard could not be happier. Looking back, the former lawyer sees how stressed and exhausted he was from his practice. He acknowledged even when we first worked with him that he had no time for his personal life. He described how he couldn't so much as take a few hours on the weekend to play his piano because his phone wouldn't stop harassing him. And yet he was hanging on to that career with a death grip. Letting go felt like a jump into the void because he couldn't see what or who he would be if he didn't do what he had been doing for more than half his life.

Yet I'll say it again: at first, Howard felt uncomfortable moving toward these new ideas. He harbored many moments of self-doubt and struggle, which is to be expected when moving toward something brand new. He constantly pushed himself out of his comfort zone, and we helped him blaze his trail incrementally. As enthralled as he surely was by his bright encore prospects, he also navigated plenty of reluctance.

Howard is an excellent example of someone who was profoundly identified with his career and superb at what he did. He enjoyed a great deal of perceived personal success. Perhaps as a result, he had such tunnel vision that he really couldn't see a future for himself. Add to that his turbulent feelings about the organization he had helped build for so many years, and the picture takes on certain ambivalences. For us, Howard Marks will always be a classic case of someone who knew he wanted an energizing future but felt very attached to his current self. Three years later, he was thriving. He remains a poster child for how imagining and then gradually approaching a possible self can be surprisingly powerful in opening up worlds of new opportunity.

Chapter Summary

The roles we play at work and in life have a profound influence on how we see ourselves and communicate our value to the world around us. They form part of our social identity.

Social identities matter most when we place a high value on belonging to a particular group, through which we form deep emotional connections and gain a significant amount of our validation from performing well. For these reasons, intense careers almost always create significant social identities.

As we consider letting go of a social identity as important as a career, the ability to imagine new roles in which we shine is critical to maintaining a sense of self-efficacy and a positive self-concept.

While we all have a tendency to think at any point in time that we have arrived at our final destination, in actuality, we continue to evolve throughout our lives, making the ability to imagine ourselves in the future a critical capacity.

Equally important is the willingness to embrace new mindsets, such as contribution instead of success, student instead of expert, and creator instead of reactor.

The power to imagine and approach an evolving version of yourself, your "possible self," is a combination of building on your current strengths, inhabiting new mindsets, and taking incremental steps in the direction of who you want to become.

PART THREE

---◦◦○◦—◦►○◄◦—◦◦○◦---

RETHINKING LIFE'S ARCHITECTURE

Design Guidelines for the Formerly Hectic Professional

chapter seven

CREATING STRUCTURE IN THE LAND OF THE FREE

We cannot solve our problems with the same thinking we used when we created them.

~Albert Einstein

The Appalling Thought of Free Time

As the old saying goes, "Nature abhors a vacuum," and as the old stereotype goes, retired people love golf. I suspect I know why: they can kill an entire day that way. One of the most daunting ideas our clients confront is the realization that time scarcity will no longer be their defining organizing principle. In the working life of the intense professional, time is ever short, and making it available to others is second nature. As one of our clients so eloquently put it, "We sell our availability for a living." Time often feels like a tyrant that is endlessly demanding the impossible: do more, do it now, never stop. Every idle moment is a wasted moment.

It is no wonder, then, that effective time management has become an embedded way of life for most of our clients. Living in a pressure cooker is completely familiar and oddly comfortable. Decades of hypervigilance and ultra-responsiveness have defined how to play and win the game of life. So what happens when that particular game is over, and time releases its grip on our throats and declares itself to be, well, whatever we want it to be?

In my case, as I mentioned before, I seemed to swing between states of frantic (and familiar) busyness and profound (and anxiety-producing) boredom. Pitched in a battle with time for my entire adult life, I struggled at first to see it as something available to me to use as I wished. Relaxation? Forget it. That felt like wasting time to me. And although I had no real scheduling pressures once I left my law firm behind, I still found myself creating conditions that required me to race about like a madwoman. And it makes sense, in a way—it's like having an obsolete superpower but inventing uses for it anyway.

I therefore understand it well when one of our clients sheepishly expresses this fear. It can sound like this: "What am I going to do with all this free time? Yikes, I'll have a whole week stretching in front of me and nothing to do with it!" And worse than boredom is the fear that they will fritter away their days because they don't know what else to do with them. Social psychologist Erich Fromm put it well when he said: "Modern man thinks he loses something—time—when he does not do things quickly; yet he does not know what to do with the time he gains except kill it."[9]

Introducing Time Sovereignty

Some default modes can be imported into this new life stage but not your relationship to time. The way we sum it up for those considering

---

[9] Fromm, Erich. The Art of Loving, 1956. https://ci.nii.ac.jp/ncid/BA85629792.

retirement is, "Time is about to be an abundant resource." As we often explain to our clients, this doesn't mean you cease to think about how to use time, but rather that you don't need to manage it as a scarce property. If you attack life as if you don't have enough time when, in reality, you do, your perceptions will swing between overwhelm and ennui. You'll feel you must do everything that ever had to get done right this minute, or you'll wander about aimlessly because you're not overwhelmed, and there's nothing to keep your adrenalin going. Either way, these old patterns no longer work in the land of the free. What, pray tell, is the alternative?

Let me digress for a moment to propose what might be a novel paradigm: that we are the ultimate arbiters of how we experience time. Time is not something that happens to us but rather the lens through which we experience life. For real world evidence of this, consider the subjective plasticity of time in the following examples. Thirty seconds can feel like an eternity if you're running wind sprints. And yet, an entire day with a new love will fly by in a flash. As do three hours when working to hit a deadline. We say, "Where does the time go?" Our experience of time literally expands and contracts according to our own perceptions.

Why might this be? Various studies have shown that both the emotional feeling we have (positive or negative) and the level of stimulation we feel (how worked up or calm we are) can influence how we perceive time and remember events.

In one study,[10] researchers asked study participants to estimate the passage of time after seeing images with known emotional qualities and excitement levels. The results showed that the emotional quality (positive or negative) and the level of excitement (measured by things like perspiration and heart rate), when considered together, had a significant impact on the perception of how much

---

[10] Alessandro Angrilli, Paolo Cherubini, Antonella Pavese, and Sara Manfredi, "The Influence of Affective Factors on Time Perception," *Perception and Psychophysics* 59 (1997): 972–982.

time had passed. For example, boring, negative images created a shorter perception of time than boring, positive ones. However, for highly exciting pictures, negative images seemed to last longer than positive ones.

In simple terms, our experience of time seems to be tied, at least in part, to how much focus we are giving to any specific moment—because of how connected we are emotionally and how attentive we are mentally to what is occurring. Of course, the quantitative amount of time that has passed in all cases is the same.

With this understanding in mind, we can begin to play with the idea that we are sovereign over time and how we use and experience it. How liberating! We can become time's master and not its servant. When we cease hurrying, we begin to enjoy the sensation of being present for even the simplest things. Instead of reacting to perceived obligations out of instinct, we can begin choosing what to do, when to do it, and at what level of priority and speed to do it. Rather than an exhausting taskmaster, time becomes a structuring tool for life. We can start to shape and define the patterns of our days, weeks, and even years into a suitable structure that organizes our time in a way that enhances the way we experience our lives.

Walk Me through Your Perfect Day

When we met with Andrew, he had already retired from his elevated position at one of the world's best-known investment banks. He came to us with a growing sense of discomfort about his experience of retirement. Four months in, he found himself wandering into his home office every day without enough to do. "I fritter the time away because I don't know where else to be or what else to do," he told us. Andrew's malaise was so real you could almost touch it. Instead of being able to say, "I'm right where I ought to be," he sounded utterly defeated as he wondered, "Why am I just sitting here killing time at my desk?" What he was used to doing was charging hard all day. He was still trying to live the same pattern with no content to support it. It was time for Andrew to start establishing new rhythms and structure.

We asked Andrew to engage in one of our favorite thought experiments. "Walk us through your perfect day," we said. "You can make this up any way you want." Andrew looked at us with a blank stare. "Huh? That's a terrifying thing you just said to me! I don't know what making it up any way I want even means."

"No problem," we say. "Start at the moment you rise and take it bit by bit. Really design it in a way that you would enjoy it as it unfolds but also reach the end of the day thoroughly pleased with what you got done. When were you mentally focused? When were you social? When were you exercising?"

Interestingly, Andrew could describe his ideal morning easily: "Rise early but with no alarm, make a delicious cup of coffee, walk out back with the dog, and watch the sunrise. Then catch up on current events before having a light breakfast." On a perfect day when he was in control of his time, he'd next head out for a hike at a nearby trail and then finish off with a short stint in the gym. As he described this morning, he seemed almost wistful. We asked him if this morning was something he was currently living, given that he was actually retired and free from the demands of his prior schedule. He looked at us a bit surprised and said, "No—I wake up, make coffee, and rush into my home office to check email and then end up surfing the web until I realize I've blown two hours. It's awful." Andrew was sticking to the old pattern he was used to even though it was obsolete. He had never thought about *reshaping* that pattern.

We continued building his ideal day, and he could easily identify that he was sharpest mentally between ten a.m. and two p.m. He enjoyed being focused deeply on a project during that time but breaking in the middle for a light lunch by himself. Then he hit another wall.

His natural question was, "Well, what am I going to do in the afternoon?"

To which we answered, "Maybe you're going to call your afternoon flextime. You're going to look at your schedule at the beginning of the week and ask yourself, 'What would I love to do this week? Whom would I love to see? What experiences do I want to have?'" He'd been telling us his regrets about living in Manhattan but never having time to take advantage of all the city's cultural opportunities. Now he took in our suggestion and said, "Okay, maybe on Monday afternoon I'll link up with my daughter and take her kid to the park. Tuesday, I'll see a museum exhibition. Wednesday, I'll go do a long yoga session." And so on.

This idea of creating a defined band of flextime is just one example of establishing a structure that provides enough definition to be approachable but also enough flexibility to permit some freedom and spontaneity. The very boundaries imposed by structure help create space for fun and freedom. Wide-open undefined nothingness makes it difficult for most people to make choices. It's too overwhelming.

A Deep Life

This phenomenon of defining structure for how we use our times dovetails with a marvelous concept of how to live a "deep life," developed by Cal Newport, a computer science professor at Georgetown University. In his best-selling book *Deep Work: Rules for Focused Success in a Distracted World*, Newport introduces the concept of "deep work" as follows: "Professional activities performed in a state of distraction-free concentration that push your cognitive capabilities to their limit. These efforts create new value, improve your skill, and are hard to replicate." He contrasts deep work with "shallow work" or "non-cognitively demanding, logistical-style tasks, often performed while distracted."

Beyond the domain of work, Newport expands this concept more broadly to address how to live a deep life. I find his structure fascinating, and I frequently bring it up with my clients as one model for thinking about how to design satisfying rhythms into days, weeks, months, or years.

Newport posits that in order to live a deep life, you need to invest your time and efforts intentionally into four concrete categories. These categories are:

1. Constitution (health and well-being)
2. Community (family, friends, collaborators)
3. Craft (work and high-quality leisure)
4. Contemplation (matters of the soul, your inner life)

What I find interesting about this paradigm is that it allows you to think about where you put your time, energy, and intention and whether those investments are enhancing—or detracting from—your experience in the four areas.

Newport advises scheduling one's day in blocks. Being aware of your biological rhythms will affect how you allocate your time. Perhaps you'll find yourself saying, "I really am sharpest in the morning, so I'm going to protect my mornings for my craft." This may involve performing a hobby or perhaps it's a class you'll be taking, or maybe the work you're doing for a nonprofit you care about. Whatever the pursuit, you'll want to earmark the most conducive time for that aspect of your life. Designing the most positive schedule for well-being provides another example of how deep living works. "I love being physical and using my body in the afternoons," you may conclude. "That's when I'm going to take that bike ride or that walk." Or maybe you most enjoy being social around meals. In that case, what will snap into place for you might involve lunches or dinners with friends or family.

You can perform this big-picture exercise by noticing connections in your life. For instance, you may ask yourself, "Am I adding to my community richness with this choice?" It's a way to become aware of the extent to which you are shaping your retirement ideas the way you truly want them to be. So much of how people conceptualize these choices takes place unconsciously because of the monolithic career they've had and the need to prioritize it over almost everything else.

The deep living paradigm offers just one approach to creating a new set of rules for structuring your life. You can ask yourself intentionally where you want to put your energy and attention and why. As I mentioned before, one of the big shifts many must make upon retiring is moving from reactor to creator. As a creator, you're the one who has to define, shape, and create, and you need a starting point from which to engage. You need some design guidelines.

Is There a Better Fuel than Fear?

As is likely clear by now, we tend to work with driven, high-performing people. By all usual external measures, they are successful. In particular, they are exceptional at meeting or exceeding the expectations of others. No surprise, then, that we spend some time digging into our clients' core motivators to consider how those motivators might shape their approach to life after an intense career.

When we asked one highly successful private equity manager what drove him to maintain his current pace, he shot back without hesitation, "Oh, that's easy. Fear." Mike was well known by his colleagues as relentless in both his ambition and his ability to persist in the face of seemingly impossible demands. He elaborated,

"Every day when I pull into my parking space, I sit there for a minute and wonder if today is the day that everyone realizes I don't belong here. I have to be superhuman as far as I'm concerned, or I won't be there at all."

Mike is just one example of the many outwardly successful people we coach who secretly worry that they are just one mistake away from being discovered as a fraud—what is widely known in psychology circles as imposter syndrome. Imposter syndrome, or IS, is common among high-achieving people and manifests as hidden self-doubt regarding some core aspect of self, such as intellect, skill, or ability. Underneath it is an essential fear of losing approval, security, or belonging—all very existential threats. And even in the absence of true IS, the motivation profile of most professionals includes a measure of fear. Pressure, exhaustion, and deadlines create a perfect storm for mistakes, and fear of making them is often the extra power boost beneath high performance. While fear can clearly be a strong motivator, its residue can also be hard to live with.

As someone like Mike approaches retirement, using fear as fuel begins to feel especially problematic. Without constant pressure to induce specific moments of panic that then drive immediate action, fear as a motivator can quickly become chronic free-floating anxiety. With nothing to conquer, all that fuel has nowhere to go.

We propose considering a different fuel source to high performers who are shifting into a less intense life. Instead of organizing life around the fear of screwing up, why not organize it around the idea of maximizing the amount of energy you have? I came upon this profound insight when I read the 2003 bestseller *The Power of Full Engagement: Managing Energy, Not Time, Is the Key to High Performance and Personal Renewal*. After studying thousands of world-class athletes and other individuals in high-pressure roles, performance psychologist James Loehr and writer Tony Schwartz concluded that "Performance, health, and happiness are grounded in the skillful management of energy." They remind the reader that "the number of hours in a day is fixed, but the quantity and quality of energy available to us is not." It turns Einstein's famous $E = MC^2$ into an equation for performance enhancement by mapping out how to build energetic capacity in service of optimal performance, health, happiness, and balance—or what they call "full engagement."

As someone who likes to have specific goals on the table at all times, this idea seized me and ultimately transformed how I live my life. I stopped pushing myself beyond capacity in every area and embraced the natural rhythms and oscillations nature gives us. For me, it was often as simple as "changing the channel," so to speak. When one activity became draining, I'd do something else equally important, but just different. I gravitated toward waking up early for contemplation prior to my children needing my attention. Then, once they were off to school, I exercised and did the work that required deep thinking. I designed my afternoons to satisfy my need for social or outdoor time. Admin tasks got batched to Saturday mornings. My energy skyrocketed.

We recommend reading *The Power of Full Engagement* to every client we meet, but a brief review here will be helpful to anyone considering new ways to shape life and fuel performance. Starting with the basics, Loehr and Schwartz tell us that we have four fundamental sources of energy:

- Physical (the quantity of our energy, high to low)
- Emotional (the quality of our energy, positive to negative)
- Mental (our ability to focus energy, distracted or attentive)
- Spiritual (the force of our energy, powerful or powerless)

Putting them together, then, we can actively work toward being physically energized, emotionally connected, mentally focused, and spiritually aligned with a purpose beyond ourselves. What we see when people start getting intentional about building capacity in these areas of energy is that their well-being and sense of productivity shoot through the roof. You've also likely noticed that these four sources of energy align nicely with Newport's four categories for creating a deep life.

As *The Power of Full Engagement* points out, we build capacity just like we build a muscle: we stress it (push it to a point of discomfort) and let it recover (allow for recuperation). Along with an intentional effort to embrace experiences outside our current comfort zone, adequate rest in each of these realms becomes a priority. This can feel revelatory to professionals who are accustomed to a world in which the ability to go without sleep is almost a badge of honor. The idea is to oscillate between expending energy and recovering energy, a phenomenon observable everywhere in nature. Think of the breath, changing seasons, migration patterns, and the tides, just to name a few. Life moves in rhythms and cycles, not a straight line, and certainly not in the redlining pattern that many professionals endure.

In our coaching practice, we use Loehr and Schwartz's construct as a springboard for designing life around rhythms, habits, and routines that build energy instead of depleting it. Most of the professionals we work with have overstressed their mental and emotional selves without enough space for recovery. They push themselves for hours at a time without a break, ignoring mental and emotional signals of exhaustion. Conversely, many have undertrained their physical and spiritual selves. Pressed for time, physical health, regular exercise, and contemplative pursuits have been deprioritized or ignored altogether.

The point of exploring these dynamics is not to judge anyone's shortcomings. Rather, for professionals on the verge of retirement, it's a great opportunity to start thinking about structuring their future lives around building holistic energetic capacity. The transition allows them to stop and ask themselves, *If I were going to build capacity physically, what would that look like for me? How might I push myself to grow in my relationships? What shape might fresh intellectual challenge take?* These are almost always new and intriguing questions for our clients. "You get to make this up any way you want it now," we tell them. "So why not make it up in a way that serves your ability to flourish on all levels for as long as possible?"

I mention *The Power of Full Engagement* here to shine a light on some of the theories and ideas that undergird how we work with people to define what life could look like if they reexamine what's fueling their choices and patterns of living. In chapter 8, I will offer specific suggestions born from our experience to shape a plan for each of these energy realms. The broader point here is that retirement presents an inflection point at which, perhaps for the first time, we really can design a masterpiece of a life for ourselves. With freedom from a demanding career, we can get intentional about structuring our lives in ways that truly energize us. That's the unique opportunity.

New Metrics: Quantity or Quality?

I think it's a fair generalization to say that most people are not happy unless they are making progress in some way. Consciously or not, we humans like to chart our advancements, measuring all manner of things: money earned, hours slept, calories consumed, steps walked. Metrics are a part of how we take stock of ourselves and our efforts, and in the professional world, metrics are the very essence of achievement. They're how we understand whether we're succeeding or not. Leaving that world behind means leaving its comparative quantification.

We make a point of telling our clients, "Those metrics in working life are going away. So you'll need to come up with your own measures. How are you going to know that you're on a path that feels like it's trending in the right direction? How will you measure your progress?" Although this may seem like a cause for celebration, it generally brings distress. They will no longer be able to say, "Well, I've billed this many hours. I got promoted to this position. I hit our earnings targets for ten straight quarters. I received the biggest bonus in history." They won't get these external, quantitative validations anymore, which usually relate, in part at least, to the money they have earned.

But progress still matters, and measuring progress is inherently an aspect of being human. Part of building a satisfying life after retiring is considering new metrics by which to gauge growth and accomplishment. We propose a shift from the quantitative and comparative metrics of working life to more qualitative and subjective measures tied to overall well-being. Not surprisingly, Loehr and Schwartz provide a helpful model for this as well. Their wonderful framework offers the measure of fitness as a touchstone. The idea of fitness meets us where we are, is specific to our own unique definitions of progress, and grows with our own expanding notions of potential. What's most intriguing about the idea of fitness is its surprising applicability beyond the realm of physical capacity.

As Loehr and Schwartz note, there are four aspects of fitness that are familiar to us when we're talking about the physical body: strength, flexibility, endurance, and resilience. Let's touch base with the familiar definitions.

- Strength—the power to push or pull against resistance with adequate force
- Flexibility—the ability to extend or stretch yourself into space
- Endurance—the ability to persist over time
- Resilience—the ability to bounce back or recover from a setback or injury

It's interesting to apply those terms to taking stock of our emotional, mental, and spiritual lives. As an example, consider what these indicia of fitness might mean in the realm of emotional energy—primarily expressed through our relationships:

- Am I emotionally strong and stable when I encounter resistance?
- Am I flexible enough to feel emotional discomfort?

- Can I endure though emotional challenges calmly and confidently?
- Can I bounce back and repair a relationship after a conflict?

Once we start asking these questions, we can move on to authentic acknowledgment. *Well, I'm not very flexible in my relationships. Things always have to be my way. That's something I can work on. Let me try to stretch myself a little.* Pushing past the edges of our emotional comfort zone will almost certainly open up opportunities to become more emotionally "fit," whatever that means for us at that particular time or in that particular relationship.

What I love most about the approach of fitness as a new measure is the fluidity and personal subjectivity of the concept. There's no black-and-white continuum to notch yourself against—you can always work on your energetic capacities and refine them to match your personal objectives and intentions. Fitness honors the fact that we're all evolving. What fitness means in one decade may be different from what it means in another. Fitness at sixty can mean something very different than it meant at twenty, and therefore, it calls us to continually live in possibility rather than assuming our best is behind us.

The findings of Loehr and Schwartz have been instrumental in molding our program. They've contributed new and compelling ways for human beings to think about the shape of their lives, why they're here, and how to expand their capacity. Best of all, the paradigm they've elaborated has allowed us to probe our clients' potential for continuing to grow in ways that improve the lives of others. Our clients like the framework immensely. It's intellectually stimulating; it's grounded in research; and it assumes the potential to continue growing as a human being rather than defaulting into a life of pure leisure or, worse, throwing in the towel on the way to a wretched decline.

Tools for Sculpting Life

In any creative project, the right tools can make the difference between a chaotic mess and a sublime masterpiece. So it is with the creative project of shaping life after the defining structure of a demanding career drops away. What follows is a tool kit of sorts for those who want to sculpt their lives into things of beauty.

A Tool Kit for Sculpting Life

1. Proactive planning
2. The artist's attitude
3. Flextime, variety, and experimentation
4. Routines and habits
5. Minimizing the drudge

Proactive Planning

As Dwight D. Eisenhower so eloquently put it, "Plans are nothing; planning is everything." Most busy professionals wearily recount story after story of disrupted plans: vacations spent in hotel business centers, arriving late to a child's performance, missing a meaningful night out with friends. The notion of a plan almost elicits laughter—as if the plan itself is an invitation from some devious force to throw in the proverbial wrench.

For this reason, plans have come to feel almost pointless to some of our clients. And yet, proactive planning is the foundational tool of intentional living. Looking ahead to decide how you'd like to live is very different from passively meandering through the week, waiting to see what shows up. And while plans themselves will always be subject to disruption, the act of planning is what makes the difference.

For this reason, we are big fans of staying involved with your calendar after retirement, not as a servant to its content but instead using it as a planning tool. Rather than be appalled by all the white space, place yourself at the end of the coming week and ask:

- If this is a spectacular week, what's happened?
- Who have I seen? What have I accomplished?
- How many times did I get to the gym?
- Did my spouse and I do something enjoyable together?

Allow your mind to let go the constraints of a work schedule and get your hands in the clay. As you generate answers to these questions, block space on your calendar to accommodate your desired outcomes. Make the reservations you need; invite the friend you'd like to see to lunch; reserve an afternoon for the art exhibit you read about last week.

The benefit of planning is twofold. The more obvious benefit is the rich life experience you can create for yourself and those around you, even assuming the occasional disruption of specific plans. The less obvious benefit is the practice of creativity itself. What feels foreign at first quickly becomes an energizing exercise in playing with possibility.

One the most powerful tools we use in proactive planning is a simple (though comically large) sheet of laminated paper called an annual planning calendar. We send one to every client and recommend they use it to plan an entire year in advance. In our world of limited screen real estate, we can barely visualize a week, much less an entire year. But zooming out to consider what you want to have seen, experienced, and accomplished in the coming year can be revelatory. We suggest starting with the knowns: for example, holidays, existing commitments, birthdays, and events you plan to attend. Place these on the calendar, and then notice the opportunities that emerge within these boundaries. Consider how the seasons effect where you want to be and when. Where would you like to travel, given what you already know about the coming year? And when does it make sense to tackle a project that requires you to be home? This level of proactive planning puts you in the position of mapping out your intentions, and if plans need to change, you can still see the big-picture goals you have and adjust accordingly.

The Artist's Attitude

While many of our clients allege that they do not have a creative bone on their bodies, we point out that they have used plenty of creativity in their working lives. The problem is not a lack of creativity; rather it is where one starts the creative process. For a typical professional, creativity is relevant as a tool for solving another's problem. A problem or challenge is presented by a client or situation, and the professional works within the form of the problem to design a solution—often a truly creative, nonobvious solution. Those are some of the stories our clients enjoy sharing the most.

What our clients are often less practiced in is creating from inception. How does one approach a blank canvas or a block of marble? That is an entirely different kettle of fish. Our suggestion is to reorient one's attitude to that of an artist and consider the core elements of artistic design: rhythm, pattern, balance, proportion, and variety, for example. As applied to the idea of planning a truly beautiful day, how could those elements be used to inform the shape of such a day?

We've already examined some novel ideas for considering daily rhythms. Both Newport's deep life model and Loehr and Schwartz's full engagement model propose thinking of the day in terms of energizing cycles and rhythms—not a linear grind to exhaustion. With this idea in mind, how do the concepts of balance and proportion organize those rhythms? For some, several hours of physical activity are essential to an enjoyable day while, for others, a thirty-minute walk in nature would be quite enough. An extrovert might require at least one dynamic social interaction a day while a more introverted person might crave solitude and more time to read or reflect. The point here is to get into the artist's mindset and be intentional about what you are designing, rather than defaulting to the way you have previously structured your life. When are you mentally sharpest? Maybe that's when you plan for a two-hour block of focused work. When do you love to be out and about? What's ideal for mealtime? Just because you've eaten lunch at your desk for twenty years does not imply that web surfing with a sandwich is the optimal plan.

Flextime, Variety, and Experimentation

As much as we encourage creating structure as part of intentional life redesign, we also warn against becoming overscheduled or rigid in thinking about how to use your newly abundant time. So much of the possibility and joy in this next chapter of life arise from the newfound freedom presented by retiring from an intense career. As an antidote to the lure of a densely packed calendar, we suggest incorporating the concept of "flextime" that we proposed to Andrew, mentioned earlier in this chapter. The idea consists of protecting a band of time every day, or at least several times a week, to engage in something novel, enjoyable, and purely for the experience itself. Flextime is like built-in permission to do those things you just never get around to doing. Not the unpleasant chore or the tedious project, but those things that have intrigued you for years but never get airtime. Like an interesting lecture that catches your eye or the ceramics studio you've wondered about forever. Flextime helps loosen up the mind, activate creativity, and get you back into the mode of exploring the world. It is a terrific avenue for introducing variety and experimentation into your life.

The benefits of this approach are documented in a fascinating 2020 study by clinical psychologist and neuroscientist Dr. Aaron Heller and his team showing that getting out in the world to experience new things can be a mood elevator.[11] Heller's study tracked 132 participants' daily GPS coordinates over three to four months to assess "experiential diversity" on a given day; a higher geolocation score reflected visiting more locations and spending meaningful time at those locations, translating into a day with lots of variety. This method, previously used successfully in animal studies, aimed to determine if daily movement and variety, while accounting for factors like location, day of the week, and temperature, could accurately predict for better moods in humans. Participants provided daily reports of their positive and negative emotions via smartphones.

The data revealed that positive emotions were higher on days when participants had a greater geolocation score (more experiential diversity), indicating that daily exposure to new things is linked to improved well-being. Heller and his team also explored whether this relationship has knock-on effects, and they found that experiential diversity and the resulting positive emotions on one day seemed to improve the odds of having more novel and diverse experiences on the following day. The pursuit of experiential diversity, then, just might be part of creating an "upward spiral" of positive emotion and improved mood. Bring it on.

Flextime also offers the opportunity to play with experimentation. If you have been in a profession in which getting it right is what you are paid to do, the idea of experimentation might be foreign indeed. But experiments are, in essence, just information-gathering exercises. They do not "succeed" or fail." They merely provide data that verifies or disproves a hypothesis. You might experiment, for example, with taking a course on creative writing. Maybe several classes into it, you discover it is not energizing you. Perfect—the

---

[11]   Aaron S. Heller, Tracey C. Shi, C.E. Chiemeka Ezie, Travis R. Reneau, Lara M. Baez, Conor J. Gibbons, and Catherine A, Hartley, "Association between Real-World Experiential Diversity and Positive Affect Relates to Hippocampal–Striatal Functional Connectivity," *Nature Neuroscience* 23 (2020): 800–804.

data is in—no more of that! You are free to stop going. But maybe you met an interesting collaborator along the way, and now you have the start of your own writers' group. Or, at the very least, you ruled out an avenue that just doesn't work for you.

When I get into my own rut and need a reminder about the fun of flextime, I revisit this quote from Salvador Dali taped to my desk: "Every morning upon awakening, I experience an exquisite pleasure: that of being Salvador Dali, and I ask myself, wonderstruck, what prodigious thing will he do today, this Salvador Dali." Let's go.

Routines and Habits

If variety and experimentation are the spice of life, then routines and habits are the meat and potatoes. Studies abound on the importance of routines and habits to our ability to execute life's requirements efficiently, and they are also linked to better overall mental health. While distinct from each other, they are interrelated concepts that share the characteristic of repetition. In a sense, together, they form the foundations of our life structure. Let's take a look at the subtle but important differences between them.

Routines are a set of actions or activities that we perform regularly and in a specific order. They are often structured and follow a schedule or a sequence. Routines can show up all over the place: consider morning routines, exercise routines, or evening routines. They provide a sense of organization and structure to our days. As you contemplate a major life change like retirement, it can feel as if every major routine in life is about to be scrambled. But on closer examination, that is not always the case. For example, we like to ask clients to tell us about their morning and evening "bookends" to the workday—what they like about them and what they'd change if they could. Many people relate that they truly love their current morning and evening routines, to which we reply, "Perfect—don't change a thing!" Keep doing what works for you. If during working life, you liked to rise early to have an hour of solitude before the day gets going, continue that practice. On the other hand, if your evening bookend started later than you would have liked because of work demands, here is an opportunity to modify it somewhat but keep the content of cooking dinner to music with your spouse. The point is to become conscious of the importance of routines and the ability to craft them in a way that serves you.

While routines are a connected sequence of conscious activities, habits are behaviors or actions that are performed automatically and regularly, often without conscious thought. Habits are formed through repetition and reinforcement and act almost like algorithms, causing us to inevitably repeat behaviors (even the ones we'd like to stop). And thank goodness for our ability to develop habits; otherwise, we'd have to consciously plan every single action we take during the day, which would exhaust our ability to do much more than survive. However, because habits can be both good for us (e.g., exercising daily) and not so good for us (e.g., smoking), and because they can develop intentionally and unintentionally, they are worthy of careful examination. James Clear, the best-selling author of the book *Atomic Habits: An Easy and Proven Way to Build Good Habits and Break Bad Ones*, provides unparalleled guidance about the power of habits to shape who we are, along with science-backed advice on how to form good habits and lose the bad ones. A pattern disrupter like retirement provides an especially ripe opportunity to examine our habits and think intentionally about how to rebuild these powerful tools of automation in service of who we want to become in this next chapter.

Minimizing the Drudge

In 1955, British historian Cyril Northcote Parkinson penned a witty essay for *The Economist*, drawing from his time in the British civil service. In this essay, the opening line gave birth to what is now known as Parkinson's Law: "Tasks will stretch to occupy the time allocated for their completion." We still chuckle about this truth decades later because it invariably proves itself out. Life is filled with all sorts of tasks, many of which, though necessary, feel like drudgery and take an inordinate amount of our discretionary time. As space and time open up in the void of an intense career, it can be easy to fill one's days with a jumble of errands, administrative tasks, and deferred chores that lack any deeper meaning than a fleeting sense of productivity. Of course, these things must get done, but we propose applying the tools of batching, delegation, and outsourcing where possible to ensure that life after retirement doesn't become an exercise in managing the mundane. After all, is that the life anyone has worked so hard for?

By batching, we mean doing similar tasks as a "batch" at the same time. For example, perhaps in this new chapter, you no longer obsessively check email. Of course, in working life, responsiveness has likely been mandatory, and every email required your attention the minute it hit the inbox. However, there is a cost to your energy and attention when you have to stop what you are doing (whether it be reading, conversing, walking in nature, eating a nice meal) to read, process, and decide whether and how to deal with an email. A batching alternative might mean checking your email twice a day and dealing with everything in the inbox during these two designated time periods. Another opportune area for batching is bill paying. Rather than pay each bill as it arrives, set aside one thirty-minute window each week to pay them all at once. In that way, you avoid ramping your process up and down repeatedly, keeping your attention free for other pursuits. Batching can be used in all sorts of life management contexts, and it can be a great way to minimize the time spent on unfulfilling chores or activities.

Similarly, delegation and outsourcing are terrific tools for off-loading jobs, tasks, or roles that you simply dislike or that someone else can handle more efficiently. Many of our clients feel a sense of responsibility to pick up some of the slack on the home front now that they are free of work pressure. That makes sense, of course, but there is an opportunity to examine how that might happen beyond simply applying their time and energy directly to the problem. For example, one client acknowledged that he had begun tutoring his son in middle school math, and both of them ended up a wreck at the end of each session. While his son needed the tutoring and our client had the skill, the entire exercise was putting a strain on their relationship. We suggested that perhaps an outside tutor was a better solution. It was a bit of a light-bulb moment for our client, who was used to jumping in and taking care of things himself. But, in this case, outsourcing that particular job was better for everyone.

This idea can be applied to all sorts of administrative and home management activities. The starting point is to inventory what needs to be done routinely and then consider whether those items are most efficiently done by you or someone else. Are there affordable ways to off-load certain tasks? Can certain items be batched into single daily, weekly, or monthly windows? These are questions worth asking when considering how to sculpt this next chapter into something magnificent.

Chapter Summary

Having worked under a model of time scarcity for decades, it can be intimidating to imagine vast stretches of free time. There is a general concern that free time will translate into boredom.

Rather than experiencing time as an external force that happens to us, we can shift our perspective and engage with time as something we control. By emphasizing our presence, connection, and attention to any given moment or activity, we can influence the way we experience time, shifting into a condition of time sovereignty.

Consider new ways to structure days by considering what would be truly ideal. Without the structural assumptions imposed by working life, one can design an ideal day by establishing new rhythms around physical activity, social engagement, mental focus, and reflection.

While many of us in working life are fueled by pressure and fear of mistakes, the inflection point of retirement offers the opportunity to consider a different way to drive performance by building energetic capacity. By focusing on enhancing physical, emotional, mental, and spiritual energy, we can design life patterns that truly energize us.

Metrics of progress are important to human satisfaction. We propose using qualitative measures and assessing your strength, flexibility, endurance, and resilience across various areas of life.

Practical tools and approaches can help you rebuild life structures in retirement. We suggest experimenting with proactive annual planning; bringing an artist's attitude to your thinking; introducing flextime; building positive routines and habits; and using tactics like batching, delegation, and outsourcing to minimize time spent on unfulfilling tasks.

chapter eight

FLOURISHING IN THE LAND OF OPPORTUNITY

To be in hell is to drift; to be in heaven is to steer.

~ George Bernard Shaw, Pygmalion

Finding New Purpose in the Face of Financial Freedom

There is a subtle but important paradox gnawing at our clients' peace of mind as they think about retirement, and it has to do with the all-important notion of having a defining purpose that drives direction and action. Without that purpose, any of us can feel adrift. For nearly everyone we coach, being a provider and building financial security have served as fundamental sources of purpose since they started their working lives. So what does it mean to face the reality that this purpose has been fulfilled—that all the work and diligent saving have, in fact, created a condition of true financial freedom? Shouldn't there be a sense of elation? For many, there is not.

Retirement can trigger a deep and confusing financial anxiety. "I won't be earning a living anymore," clients will tell me in a discernable key of distress. Yet rationally, they know they have amassed more than a comfortable nest egg. In our experience, there are a couple of keys to solving this puzzle.

First, I'll revisit a feature of the American worker and the conditioning we receive about saving money. Particularly since the advent of the 401(k), we've been trained to save from the moment we started working. The danger of spending more than we're bringing in is pounded into our psyches before we've even taken our first vacation as a working adult. We learn that spending more than we earn is irresponsible, a mistake, if not a flaw in our character. Now, suddenly, retirement requires us to overcome that trained response. As we explain to our clients, you must shift from a *saver* to a *spender*.

It's time to embrace the notion that you squirreled away a lifetime of nuts so that one day you could finally eat them. A new purpose appears on the horizon, beyond that of provider. As I noted in chapter 7, the opportunity to find new metrics to measure growth and progress, beyond expanding one's net worth, emerges. This single pivot is a critical moment of transformation. The way forward is to shift from the mindset of a saver to being comfortable spending— but, critically, the spending must be aligned with new purposes that are meaningful. That is to say, we must reshape our belief system around money and get very clear about what purposes (beyond mere security) have been enabled by the money that has been saved. It is for this reason we spend time with our clients helping them answer just this question.

Our favorite inquiry is to explore what money represents to a client beyond safety and security. For example, does it represent:

- A way to care for others?
- Access to enjoyable experiences?
- A source for charitable giving?
- A way to empower opportunity?
- All these things?

As we map the contours of possibility, we can often see anxiety turn to excitement about the many ways abundant financial resources can fuel new areas of purpose and meaning. The emerging attitude might sound something like this: *Well, it's actually appropriate that I'm spending, since the whole point of saving was to draw on it one day. This means that I can help my niece with her college tuition and also provide a safety net for my mother if she needs it. And we can take some of the big trips we've never managed to make happen.*

As these ideas take shape, we propose that our clients dig into their financial positions at a more granular level than has previously been necessary. We suggest a concept called "permission budgets" that are designed around the most important purposes for their financial resources. If travel is one, then we propose earmarking a certain dollar amount per year so the money is already "spent" in the overall game plan. A similar approach can be taken with charitable giving and areas of planned family support. In this way, it is possible to analyze the long-range effects of spending these resources along the way and adjust accordingly. It avoids the decision fatigue of wondering whether these expenditures make sense every time the need or opportunity arises.

Other important aspects of this analysis include debunking the false assumptions many of us have when we think about our retirement accounts. For one, we imagine that our patterns of spending and consumption at age eighty will be the same as at sixty. We also imagine that we will want to maintain the same portfolio of real estate twenty years from now. The reality is that most people begin to "rationalize the empire" as they age by selling second properties or downsizing into smaller homes. As we age, the footprint of our lives does tend to shrink and our spending along with it. Finally, many assume they will never again make money. We remind people that retirement does not necessarily mean an end to earning power. No one we work with wants a life of pure leisure for the next thirty years, and while they might struggle at first to see the array of opportunities for continued engagement, we know from experience they are abundant and, in many cases, remunerative.

Personal Fulfillment: The Pursuit of Meaning

As I've noted throughout this book, the ability to pursue purpose and meaning are core to human satisfaction. As motivational speaker and writer Denis Waitley puts it, "It is not in the pursuit of happiness that we find fulfillment, it is in the happiness of pursuit." Knowing this, many people come to us with default ideas about how to stay engaged after they retire from their primary careers. These default ideas almost always lie adjacent to their current professional identities. In the case of lawyers, for example, they arrive with plans like:

- I'll become a mediator.
- How about an arbitrator?
- Teaching law school is something I could do.

Serving as a director on a corporate board is another common placeholder goal. In actuality, they usually have not analyzed whether any of these roles would be truly interesting or bring forward the aspects of their working lives that created a sense of purpose, meaning, and fulfillment. But these sensible ideas serve up a ready answer when asked by all and sundry, "So, what are you going to do next?" Standing on the brink of retirement, "I don't know" feels like a pitiful response.

Because everyone faces the question "What will you do?" when they go public with their retirement date, we try to inoculate our clients against this external pressure. We tell them to consider the motives of their interrogators. More than an urge to probe your future plans, we say, their inquiry is as much for themselves and their own peace of mind. They want to see that you've got it figured out, so when they cross that threshold, they too will have figured it out. With the heat on you to have a satisfactory answer to the big question, it's very easy to grab at the most obvious opportunities because they seem to assuage mutual anxieties and make sense. We are actually big fans of having a ready response to that relentless inquiry (sort of like an elevator pitch), but don't let your easy response limit your effort to find true fulfillment in your next chapter. Instead, we tell our clients that everything should be a "no" unless it's a "hell, yes!"

Beyond the surface need for an elevator pitch, we work hard to help people avoid staking their future fulfillment on canned solutions. In most cases, deeper digging reveals that those solutions aim too low. What we're trying to help people do is to analyze who they are, what they're about, and how they can be the author of their own lives. This doesn't mean that every idea anyone comes to us with lands in the trash bin. But it does mean that they remain just ideas until we validate them together. To quote the Renaissance master Michelangelo, "The greater danger for most of us lies not in setting our aim too high and falling short, but in setting our aim too low and achieving our mark."

Carolyn came to us already fourteen months into her retirement. She had confidently left her position with a major management consulting firm, excited about her next chapter. She and her husband had grand plans to travel, and she looked forward to making a difference in the realm of education. In fact, she had always loved the aspects of her role that required teaching, training, and mentoring and figured she'd enjoy taking that piece forward.

But Carolyn was surprised and confused by her general sense of malaise now that she was fully into her new life. She had leveraged a professional connection almost right away and landed a spot as an adjunct professor at a well-known university, teaching an evening course in business management twice a week. Well into her second semester, she felt frustrated and more than a little distressed that she was not finding fulfillment in the experience.

In order to get ahead of just this sort of situation, we work with our clients to develop a summary of characteristics that would ideally be present in any future endeavor they choose to pursue. The idea behind this exercise is to disaggregate a professional's core aptitudes from the specific tasks and responsibilities that featured in their career. When reading the resulting list, one wouldn't know if the person being profiled was a lawyer, a doctor, or whatever specialized service provider they are.

To start with, we ask for stories that align with our clients' most fulfilling periods of working life: "Think of a time in your professional life when you couldn't wait to get into the office and roll up your sleeves. A time when you were energized. Tell me about the people, the kinds of problems you were solving, the pace, your role, the outcomes." Such goads are designed to focus less on retro-checking the boxes of what they did than on fashioning an affecting narrative of the circumstances in which they felt most energized and engaged.

We're listening for themes that inspire and animate. We're listening for what lights people up. From these cascading sequences of revelation, we then extrapolate the common denominators of fulfillment that engage both heart and mind. What results is a profile of the characteristics that are likely to support true fulfillment, recognizing that the future contexts will look very different from the previous ones. To borrow from executive coach Marshall Goldsmith, what got them here isn't going to get them there.

In Carolyn's case, her most fulfilling work experiences indeed centered around opportunities to teach and train others. She loved watching the light bulb go on and supporting people as they developed new skills and capacities. She was masterful at crafting intensive workshops and stimulating dynamic discussion among attendees. She also enjoyed the sense of accomplishment that came from regular cycles of completion—she showed up, went deep for a defined period of time, and then tied up her work.

When we drilled down on her current teaching role and compared it to the profile of what she actually loves to do, the disconnect became obvious. Carolyn was teaching a large group of students, many of whom were taking her course to satisfy a curriculum requirement. The course required her to show up twice a week for an entire semester, and the preparation was fairly substantial. She could not seem to get the students to engage with even simple questions, much less challenge each other in conversation. So, while the broad concept of teaching was a fine idea, standing in front of a large number of relatively disengaged students behind their laptop screens—that was not even close to a "hell, yes" for Carolyn. It lacked many sparks. She experienced none of small-group engagement she loved, and it required an inordinate amount of work for almost no money. It entailed a fixed schedule that kept her from the travel she had dreamed of. And she found she had very little interaction with other professors because adjuncts are not part of the university ecosystem.

When we rolled up our sleeves with Carolyn to reshape her options for teaching, we explored the idea of designing a boot camp course, perhaps over the winter or summer term. It would be targeted to more senior students and allow for a maximum of ten enrollees. The content would be arranged to provide more student activities and less lecturing by Carolyn. She could then go deep for a couple of weeks with a small group of students who truly wanted to master the material, freeing herself up for travel the rest of the year. Suddenly, it all made sense. Teaching was not the problem; the format was—and Carolyn realized that if she was not going to love this gig, then why on earth was she trading her energy, time, and freedom to do it? Carolyn's first attempt at a fulfilling postcareer purpose was close to where she eventually landed, but by making some adjustments, she finally felt the satisfaction she craved. It would've been easy to just give up, but it's wonderful that she found a way to pivot instead.

New Forms of Meaningful Engagement

This nagging question of how to redeploy talent and skill resounds in virtually all our sessions. Perhaps nowhere did it resonate more poignantly than in our session with Rich. As global chair of his firm's banking and finance practice, Rich had also been the relationship partner for one of the firm's largest institutional clients. Year after year, he ranked as one of the top lawyers in his practice area.

All this to say Rich is a very high-performing person who sets a standard of excellence for himself. But not without cumbrous strain. Billing over three thousand hours a year for decades had left the sixty-one-year-old flatly exhausted. He attended our program fully ready to curtail his working life, yet he struggled to see how he'd put his skills to work if not at that breakneck pace. When we started dissecting his actual role in his clients' deals, we learned he was firmly at the helm, not at all in the weeds. Still, something remained unclear about the nitty-gritty of his day-to-day. We asked point blank, "What do you really do?" His answer spoke volumes: "Well, when it boils down to it, I help the young businesspeople at the bank make smart decisions. I help them think clearly, exercise good judgment, and solve problems in an effective way."

With that, our needle moved. Rich nudged us further in the right direction as he reflected on other qualities he valued in life. The towering performer surprised us by stressing the importance of cultivating mind, body, and spirit in holistic terms that could just as well as come from an enlightened guru. Here's what we suggested: "What if you went to your major client and said, 'I'm retiring from law, but I'm not going away. In fact, I'd like you guys to engage me to be a performance coach for your rising stars'?"

Rich was intrigued. He understood that such a role would allow him to control how much or how little time he would devote to the new pursuit. Better yet, he could take forward just the part of what he was doing that he enjoyed the most: helping younger rising stars grow into the roles they'd been handed. The stakes were still gratifyingly high, yet the hours and stress didn't have to be. What's more, Rich's offer to remain engaged would only strengthen his law firm's ongoing relationship with the bank. He'd be able to allay his client's fear that they'd be losing a key strategic asset with the simple reassurance, "I'll still be here to do this piece."

Were they to balk at the other aspects of his work that he'd be leaving behind, he could remind them, "There is a whole team of lawyers at the law firm who can do the legal work at the level you're used to."

I share these stories about Carolyn and Rich to offer just a couple of examples of ways highly skilled professionals approached shaping new forms of meaningful engagement that specifically align with protecting time and space for other pursuits. It is a mistake to think meaningful endeavors must also be all consuming or that unappealing trade-offs must be made to accommodate them. To the contrary, we observe that the most fulfilled among our clients prioritize their other goals—health, relationships, personal interests, or inner life—along with whatever they choose to do with their professional skills.

Health and Energy: Tapping into Unlimited Capacity

A great opportunity lies ahead when the demands of an intense career fall away—the opportunity to define and establish new goals, habits, and routines that support enduring health and high levels of physical energy. Even the relatively fit among our clients confess that their work schedules get in the way of their being as intentional as they'd like regarding their physical well-being. And it makes sense on the surface. Our clients use their minds as their primary tools of accomplishment, so spending time enhancing physical performance can seem like a distraction.

But when we ask our clients what one thing they would choose if they could have anything in this next decade of their lives, the most common response is "vibrant health." While we are not doctors or physical trainers or dieticians, we do spend time defining what vibrant health means to our clients and how they might think about prioritizing it. "Tell us about a time when you felt your absolute best physically—when you had abundant energy and considered your health to be top-notch." For those who are actively engaged in conscious health-related strategies, this exercise usually reaffirms their efforts and exposes opportunities to do even more; those who've neglected this aspect of life often take us back to their twenties or thirties and recall periods when they were regularly active and felt bulletproof physically.

As we begin to create outlines of what optimal health and energy mean to a client, we often prompt them to consider, in simplest terms, how they eat, move, and sleep. An abundance of strong science supports the notion that specific strategies in these three areas can make a huge difference in how our bodies perform and feel. Rather than accepting current physical limitations as fixed, we explore with clients what might be possible as they reclaim control over their time and schedules.

One of my favorite stories of a health turnaround is Jeremy. He came to work with us at a relatively young age, having pledged to retire at forty-nine. He'd spent nearly two decades at a large public company, rising to the role of president. His workload often felt impossible. He thought about work around the clock every day of the year. Jeremy presented with burnout in its purest form, suffering from exhaustion, alienation from his job, and a sense of diminished efficacy.

"I'm going to die at my desk—and soon—if I don't get out of there now," he declared at our initial encounter. Jeremy's stated plan was to exit the company at the end of the current fiscal year, scant months ahead. Throughout our sit-down, he never wavered in his conviction that retirement would be a relief. By his own account, he was overweight, prediabetic, and stressed out. "I can't turn my health around when I'm working twenty hours a day," he reported as if putting himself on notice. Only about 11 percent of today's workers intend to retire before age sixty (according to a 2022 Employee Benefit Research Institute survey), and Jeremy could hardly wait to join this statistic. Otherwise, he felt certain he'd end up as a different statistical outlier—one much grimmer.

While Jeremy could imagine many future aspects of his next chapter, he felt unsure how to begin. As we worked through his overall goals for the coming decade, Jeremy concluded that ne needed to reclaim his physical health as his top priority. With that clarity,

Jeremy set about redesigning his lifestyle, allowing nothing else to interfere. He attended a comprehensive health-based retreat where he received a customized plan for exercise, nutrition, sleep, and stress management. Knowing he felt motivated by deadlines and competition, he registered for a marathon six months out and structured his daily exercise toward achieving that goal. He also reported that the most transformative aspect of the medical retreat had been what he learned about food choices, glucose levels, and overall metabolic health.

> I'm someone who needs to understand the "why" behind what I'm doing. Sure—my doc has told me plenty of times to eat healthier and lose weight, but without understanding the science of how and why, that advice went nowhere with me.

Now, armed with knowledge, Jeremy was actually galvanized by his power to design a healthier diet.

Within a matter of months, Jeremy felt like a new man. He had lost thirty pounds on the way to his goal of losing thirty more, and his energy levels were reminiscent of his twenties. He was running regularly and had added two sessions a week with a strength trainer. His blood pressure was now in a normal range, as were his blood sugar levels. In Jeremy's mind, regaining his health was job one, and all future opportunities would be built on that foundation. He treated the first year after he retired as a "health sabbatical" and believes strongly that he'll never let it slide again, no matter what he chooses to do next with his professional life.

Relationships: Your Most Valuable Portfolio

Just as physical habits relating to diet, exercise and, sleep affect physical energy, our interactions with other people influence our emotional energy. Consider the difference between a day filled with positive collaboration and laughter and a day filled with conflict and aggression. For most, the former boosts our positive emotions while the latter can leave us emotionally exhausted, irritable, and disconnected. In working life, we don't necessarily get to choose all the people who populate our world, but as we gaze ahead to a life we create, we are much more in charge of that dynamic. As one client reflected to us several years after retiring, "Basically, at this stage, I get to do what I want, when I want, and most importantly, with whom I want." It is not just anecdotal evidence that underscores the importance of relationships to overall thriving.

Consider the findings of the Harvard Longitudinal Study of Adult Development,[12] one of the longest-running studies ever conducted on human development. Initiated in 1938, it has followed the lives of two groups of men (initially Harvard College sophomores and inner-city Boston boys) to investigate factors influencing physical and mental well-being across the lifespan. The study, authored by George E. Vaillant, MD, has provided valuable insights into the predictors of a fulfilling life, emphasizing the significance of relationships and personal growth to well-being in later years. Of particular note are the findings that abundant positive relationships contribute not only to emotional and psychological well-being but also to physical health, cognitive function, and overall resilience in the face of life's challenges. As the [summary box] describes in more detail and Vaillant concludes, "Before and after age 50, cultivate the richest social network you possibly can. Your life will be better for it."

---

[12] George E. Vaillant, *Triumphs of Experience: The Men of the Harvard Grant Study.* (Cambridge, MA: The Belknap Press of Harvard University Press, 2012).

How Relationships Contribute to Aging Well

Social Connections and Well-Being: Maintaining strong social connections is associated with overall well-being and happiness in the aging population.

Longevity and Social Support: Individuals with robust social networks tend to live longer, indicating that supportive relationships play a vital role in physical health and resilience as people age.

Impact on Cognitive Health: Engaging in social activities and maintaining social ties can contribute to cognitive vitality and a lower risk of cognitive decline.

Emotional Resilience: Emotional support from friends, family, and community helps individuals navigate life's challenges and enhances resilience in the face of difficulties.

Interpersonal Dynamics: The quality of relationships matters; it's not just about the quantity. Meaningful, positive, and supportive interactions with others have a more significant impact on well-being than mere social presence.

Adaptability and Growth: The research indicates that individuals who maintain active and positive social lives are more adaptable and open to growth in their later years, enhancing ongoing personal development and a sense of purpose.

For this reason, we encourage our clients to define the contours of their ideal relationship world. "Tell me who's in your world with you when it's just the way you want it" we often ask. "What's true of the dynamic you have in your key relationships when you feel the most positive emotional energy?" can be a follow up. While close family members are typically at the center, we often discover that the workplace has provided an abundant source of enriching relationships, and of all the losses retirement insinuates, the loss of these affiliations and the overall sense of community can feel hardest to replace.

When Mark sought out our program, his most pressing concern about his then-approaching retirement was the loss of his community. What stayed with me was the pensive question he articulated: "How am I going to replace this fabulous people-world I inhabit?" The reinforcement of that concern fused a pleasurable sense of involvement with a wistfulness about impending loss: "I like the work fine, but I love the people." Everything Mark felt he'd achieved during his three decades at his firm flowed from his interpersonal relationships. His greatest contributions centered on his ability to recruit outstanding lawyers and teams to the firm. He had carefully shaped and executed his office's growth strategy in this way. He was good at attracting talent because people trusted who Mark was as a human being and appreciated his genuine excitement and optimism about their potential. "I'm a fine lawyer. I can do the work. But where I'm a genius is with people" is how he put it. "I can attract them, energize them, inspire them, and have fun along the way."

As we drilled down with Mark on his life outside the firm, we learned that he had begun working sporadically with two friends who were producing craft gin in their small-batch distillery. Mark's varied assistance included designing strategies to host events to elevate awareness of and loyalty to the brand. These events had been steadily attracting more attendees and creating dedicated fans of the botanical-infused spirit. While his efforts were enjoyable and effective, this endeavor resided in Mark's mind as an amusing diversion.

Going further into the actual work he was doing with the distillery, Mark shared story after story of the new friendships he had made and the sense of camaraderie he felt with the founders. Suddenly, it hit him that what had seemed like a mere hobby could now become his new source of community. He realized, *I'm going to keep doing what I've always done in my career, but I'm going to do it to build this craft gin business.* Relief turned to excitement as he saw a way to rebuild a rich community around growth and possibility. Mark's knack for infusing even the most mundane moments with fun found fertile ground in which it could continue to flourish. It was a new and essential lease on a life grounded in relationships.

It is not just the opportunity to build new relationships that exists but the chance to revive long-standing ones. Many clients lament the dormancy of old friendships that still mean a great deal to them, imagining too much time has passed to reach out and expect much interest in return. In our experience, however, that is a false assumption. We remind our clients that these very friends likely feel the same sheepishness; everyone has been consumed in middle adulthood with matters of career and family. It is the rare person indeed who has been able to regularly prioritize friendships that are not facilitated by the convenience of a connection to their kids' school, their office, or the neighborhood. So our oldest friends have been in the same stages of life we've been in. They, like we, feel very sheepish about reaching out. With that in mind, we ask, "How would you feel if an old friend reached out to you and proposed a phone call or lunch? Would you be pleased or somehow offended?" The consistent answer is "pleased" or even "delighted," and the obvious follow-up opportunity is to start reaching out proactively to old friends. The downsides of such an exercise are minimal, but the potential upsides are limitless.

We offer a clear instruction for how to start this process. Our male clients, especially, latch onto this tactic because it's an analytical approach that feels comfortable: we invite them to simply take an inventory of all their friendships. It sounds obvious, but it is hugely helpful to do this. Make a spreadsheet, use a Word document, or just create a written list:

- Who are your oldest friends?
- Who are your newest friends?

- Who do you miss from high school? College? Law school? Sports?
- Who are the friends from your working life you hope to stay in touch with after you retire?
- Who are the members of your extended family—cousins, maybe—you have lost touch with but wish you hadn't?
- Do you have couple friends you met through school functions?

Next, notice where they are, because your approach to engaging with these individuals will be different based on whether they are local or not. Then, think about how best to reach out. It might be as simple as sending an email to get something on the calendar—for example, a fishing trip—for six months from now.

When we do this exercise with our clients, we find that all they needed from us as their guides was an idea, a starting point, and a little bit of assurance they won't be rejected. Because nurturing relationships has possibly been a blind spot, some of our clients just needed some hand-holding to get started. They often have what seems like a brain freeze, a feeling of "stuckness" in this area of life, so we help get things moving. It's fair to say men struggle with feeling stuck more than women, but the great news is that once they build a little positive momentum reaching out to old friends, they do just fine and feel a lot of excitement about the possibilities.

The last tactic I want to offer on this topic of reconnecting with friends is setting up standing plans. People love this idea. It could be a weekly lunch or pickleball game, a monthly phone call, or an annual trip. Our clients never had the freedom to make standing plans during their intense careers because they'd always be interrupted. But now things are different, and the energy to make the plan only has to be expended once as the plan is happening unless they cancel it. Standing plans are a rich approach to friendship: you get the pleasure of looking forward to the time you'll have together, the pleasure of experiencing it, and the pleasure of reflecting on how nice it was to see or talk with your friend. It's a constant loop of opportunity to appreciate the connection.

Peace of Mind: The Holy Grail of Well-Being

We all have an inner life, whether we pay specific attention to it or not. When I first considered the idea of spiritual energy as a well-spring of expanded capacity, I was both perplexed and intrigued. I began to experiment with ways of observing my own inner life, fairly certain I was far from enlightened about how my own mind worked and what stories it made up about my choices and my life. When I retired from practicing law, I was far more comfortable in the mode of achieving than being. While I had been raised within a structure that included church on Sundays, my family did not have a strong spiritual bent, and I had concluded (with no examination at all) that the point of being alive was to accomplish and succeed—whatever that meant.

As I became curious about how to develop a more intentional spiritual life, I stuck to my comfort zone, taking a squarely intellectual approach. I began to rise an hour earlier each morning, reserving that time for solitude (and coffee). I read, I wrote down my thoughts, and I became aware of how little control I had previously had over the gymnastics of my own mind and what felt like my essential purpose for existing. Eventually, meditation became a central practice for me, opening up a world I'd never explored before. The most compelling outcome for me was a newfound ability to notice my thoughts and brewing reactions to unwanted situations. I was now in the driver's seat of my mind (at least sometimes) for perhaps the first time in my life. From there, I deepened my interest in the various spiritual pathways human beings travel, incorporating regular spiritual and philosophical study into my mornings. These sixty to ninety minutes of solitude each day have become my most treasured routine.

Not surprisingly, the concepts of spiritual energy and peace of mind are the least scoped out by our clients. Of course, there's a percentage of people we work with who have highly developed spiritual lives. But the vast majority, like me when I left my practice, have not had time or attention to direct to an inner life or contemplation of any sort. We hear rumbles of their being lost in spiritual space. "I don't know how to do that, but I recognize it's an important part of being a human being," they'll say. Or "I've just never had time or made time for anything spiritual." It resembles an unexplored frontier—they know it's out there somewhere but are not sure how to approach it.

As in all our work, we tend to have a pretty intellectual conversation about all this. We start by asking if there are practices or contexts that help them achieve peace of mind. If there are no ready answers, we offer some more specific prompts. "When or where do you achieve those moments when everything just feels in sync?" Often, this question jogs loose insights like "When I'm in nature—hiking, skiing, or cycling." Or "When I'm walking along the shore at sunrise." These observations start to reveal how certain contexts can pull us into the present moment, where our senses are alive and our minds are, for a time, quieter. Nature is a common example, given its vastness and beauty.

As we probe for more, we ask our clients to identify other pathways that help provide perspective; create a sense of purpose; or offer the opportunity to observe thoughts, emotions, and internal narratives. We are not probing specifically for a God concept or a faith-based construct, although plenty of our clients relate to these aspects of spirituality. Our inquiry is simply about examining the inner life. "What robs you of your peace of mind?" we often ask. Answers like "Worrying about the future" or "Acting in a way that is not really lined up with who I want to be" are common.

We are in no way trying to tell people what direction they should go in. Rather, we propose that there is value in becoming the observer of your mind and inquiring into the nature of your existence—value in terms of examining thoughts, calming worries, and inspiring big questions. We always ask people to rate their peace of mind and then to consider how they might intentionally work on improving that rating. What results are personalized approaches to connection to some larger scheme, to grounding themselves in the here and now, and to placing their problems in perspective. Whether faith based, philosophical, meditative, or nature based, making time and space for contemplation has resounded for our clients as a worthwhile and expansive investment of time and effort.

Putting It All Together: From Monolith to Mosaic

With the notion of intentional design residing in our approach to life after retirement, we seem to land on art-related themes as helpful metaphors. The mosaic is one such example. For most, an intense career has been a sort of monolith in their lives. It certainly was in mine. It was the singular organizing principle around which all other aspects of life had to exist. Its contours and pace could change rapidly—a sudden trip overseas or an all-consuming transaction that translated into twenty-hour workdays—knocking everything around it asunder. Priorities like health, family, friends, reading, and other interests found their place tucked around the edges where and when they could fit, if at all. None of this is meant to be a complaint; careers are what they are, and dedication and commitment to them is part of what makes them so meaningful. But the very fact of their monolithic nature also implies a rather capacious void when they disappear.

For this reason, we ask our clients to consider a model for their lives that resembles a mosaic more than a monolith. The definition we like for the word *mosaic* is a "combination of diverse elements that forms a coherent whole." For most of our clients, this is an entirely new way to think about life structure. As this idea takes hold, our clients begin to reshape priorities and opportunities to create something balanced, thoughtful, and pleasing to them. They become designers of their life experience, realizing that they can use space and time to accommodate most of the new ideas, experiences, and priorities that strike them as worth exploring. As I once heard the author Elizabeth Lesser say so beautifully, "It is not either/or; it's both and more."

As we work with our clients in shaping their mosaics, we offer suggestions that have proven effective for others. For example, we love to highlight endeavors that offer double or triple bottom lines. What we mean here are activities or opportunities that enrich several aspects of life at the same time. If a client enjoys walking or running, then registering for a cause-based race with a group of friends offers the prospect of upside in the realms of health, community, and meaning. Similarly, for an aspiring author, pursuing a course in writing provides an avenue into continued learning and new relationships and a pathway to the next professional endeavor. Things like hobbies and interests can now find a meaningful home in the overall picture, as can more structured commitments like working with a trainer twice a week or volunteering with an admired organization. Opportunities abound to combine physical activities, social encounters, acts of service, continued learning, travel, spiritual quests—the possibilities are truly endless, and the experimentation can be thoroughly enjoyable.

Only recently did an observer point out to me how much of my thinking about and approach to this otherwise dry topic of retirement seems to center around the notions of art and beauty. *What an odd place for a former corporate lawyer like me to land.* Probing further, I was asked, "What's the most influential narrative you've ever read or watched—and why?" I am familiar with this technique of asking intriguing questions that force our minds to quickly identify superlatives—often serving up very revealing responses. The first answer that popped into my mind was Roberto Benigni's 1997 movie *Life Is Beautiful*, about the power of one man's human spirit despite his family's internment in a Nazi concentration camp. Pressed by my inquirer to explain the film's pull, I quickly narrowed it down to the father's unflagging ability to create, in the midst of true hell, a real and joyful world for his son through nothing more than the power of imagination. The image of (spoiler alert) the father marching to his death like a toy soldier in order to shield his boy from the horrors of his fate was unforgettable to me. He was able to embody the joy in life right up to the moment he died because he cared so much about his boy's perception of what was happening. The father's power of imagination, humor, and determination truly created his son's perceived reality. The astounding revelation for me was that it's our own thoughts, words, and actions that construct our lives and what we perceive them to be. We get to choose.

I hadn't thought of it before, but there it was: this theme is the essence of my work. Call me idealistic, but just as *Life Is Beautiful* is a story about what's possible (even in the most unwanted of circumstances), I invite my clients to join me in possibility and activate their imaginations to design the spectacular lives they want and deserve.

Chapter Summary

Humans need purpose. When the twin goals of providing for one's family and creating long-term financial security have been met, it can be challenging to connect with fresh purpose. True financial freedom enables us to deploy our economic resources in new and significant ways.

Meaningful engagement is a cornerstone of flourishing. When considering how to use career-related skills and talents in new and fulfilling ways, it is critical to avoid defaulting into "sensible" ideas that otherwise leave us flat or rob us of time and space for other priorities.

With newfound control over time and schedule and, therefore, newfound control over how we approach diet, exercise, and sleep, the pursuit of vibrant health and abundant energy can be prioritized in retirement like never before.

Relationships are among the most important aspects of aging well and ensuring a positive and resilient approach to life. Defining and shaping a robust approach to community and connection is perhaps the greatest investment opportunity presented by retirement.

Nurturing a peaceful inner life, whether through meditation, faith-based structures, study, or time in nature, is at the heart of true well-being. Retirement offers a fresh opportunity to explore the content of our minds and life's biggest questions.

As we think about assembling all the potential aspects of life in retirement, we offer the metaphor of designing a coherent and beautiful mosaic, as opposed to retaining the model of a professional monolith. We choose the pieces and how they fit together.

chapter nine

ALL TOGETHER NOW— FROM ME TO WE

It does not really matter what we expect from life, but rather what life expects from us.

~Viktor Frankl, psychologist

Getting Everyone on the Same Page

There is a wonderful proverb of disputed origin that goes something like this: "If you want to go fast, go alone; if you want to go far, go together." Within this wisdom lies an obvious truth for anyone who has come far enough to contemplate retirement: *I did not do this alone.* And, perhaps more importantly, *I am not planning to finish this journey alone.* Much of what I have explored in this book concerns the individual who is retiring, who must grapple with the enormity of how retirement changes their identity, structure, and purpose, to name only a few concerns. But equally important and often even more pressing to our clients is the jumble of concerns about how this momentous decision will affect everyone else in their world. Often, that world includes a spouse or life partner, in which case questions abound about how the client's lack of a career will change that dynamic. Perhaps there is not full agreement as to where to live in this next chapter. Perhaps there are dependent children, aging parents, or other family members who must be considered when developing plans to relocate. Then, too, years, if not decades, of professional relationships require sorting out—all the swirling unknowns of how clients will react, how younger colleagues will fare, and how work-related friendships will be affected.

Well before any specific retirement date is chosen, holistic planning affords the opportunity to bring these key people into conversations about what the change will mean for them as well as for the person retiring. Quite frequently, there are mistaken assumptions about or misalignments in pretty crucial aspects of the future that can only be addressed by digging into the goals and desires of everyone involved. Simply put, retiring is not a solo operation.

I am reminded of a consultation with Hans, a German lawyer married to Barbara, an American doctor. They had two adult daughters well into their twenties who were launched and happily independent, though living nearby. Hans was pretty excited about retirement when we spoke with him. He was already an adjunct professor at a well-respected university, and he had several other teaching offers to boot. He hugely enjoyed the classroom. So much so, in fact, that he was thinking about how to be on both sides of the lecture podium. He wanted to continue teaching and to become a student again as well.

What Hans was struggling with most involved geography. "I want to be in Germany two or three months a year so I can teach a course there," he explained. "My wife does not want to be there at all. She says, 'Well, what on Earth am I going to do there?' We're not at all on the same page."

Barbara had retired many years before. Her German was barely proficient enough to ask for directions. Language remained a major impediment for her. Hans replayed the objections she would raise whenever the topic came up: "So, you're going to be there teaching. What am I going to be doing?" Plus, he figured—all too realistically—that she didn't want to be away from her daughters for three months at a time. Hans understood Barbara's perspective. What clouded his vision was how to invite her to become part of creating a win-win solution.

Though our conversation began squarely in professional terrain, it naturally spilled into the byways of private life. Hans wondered, "Are these the kinds of things you help people with?"

"Yes," I assured him. "Couple dynamics are big in our line of work." We are not marriage counselors per se, but we certainly facilitate conversations that help couples design a plan that works for both of them. Ideally, retirement should enhance your relationship, both by opening up new ways to be together and by presenting new opportunities for independent endeavors. The important thing is to design it together.

I delved right in. "How would Barbara feel about improving her language skills?" I asked. David and I knew of an online individual language-learning platform. Barbara was not a fan of classrooms, but she hadn't thought about a one-on-one Zoom course. Though it was a promising start, pragmatic solutions can only help to an extent. On a deeper level, we observed to Hans that Barbara herself might be feeling a little lost. She gave up her career to be with her girls, and now they're grown. She needed her own inspired agenda, and she needed to see how Germany fit into that agenda.

The best way forward, we felt, was for Hans to co-create his project with her. First, he'd have to relinquish masterminding his own plan and embrace a mentality of inclusion. To reset his thinking, I suggested, "You might find it useful to move into the 'What if?' zone, away from the 'This is what we're doing' zone." I could almost hear the penny drop with this guidance. For Hans to respond so positively showed his receptivity to changing his mindset and his awareness of the need to unlock the world through Barbara's eyes. We were on to something.

I then added, "What if you made this an opportunity for your daughters to join you during part of your stay in Germany?" He had told us they both had positions that permitted them to work remotely from anywhere on the planet. Encouraged by Hans's excited nods, I ventured onward. "What if you also made this an opportunity for their significant others to join? You've got to liven up this project for everybody." The difference in planning for one and persuading another versus planning for all became increasingly apparent to Hans. He began to see how he could present the project not as purely his, but as a wonderful option that merited his wife's—indeed, the whole family's—shared consideration. "Look at Germany as a unique opportunity your family has," I counseled. "Not everybody has such a meaningful relationship with a second country."

The shift In Hans's mindset came about by directing him to view his retirement program from his wife's perspective, understand her reactions, and propose solutions that addressed them. Hans came to us saying, "I want to be in Germany every year, and it is a problem." Now he can rejoice: "We have the opportunity as a family to be in Germany every year in a deep way, not as tourists." And the cherry on top? As it turned out, Barbara's best friend in the world lived in Berlin.

Our follow-up conversations with Hans indicated that he was on a productive path. "I shared some of these ideas with Barbara and told her about your program," he said. "She's interested." In subsequent sessions, we worked with Hans and Barbara to shape their coming decade in a way that all concerned could embrace and enjoy. As business author Ken Blanchard pointedly puts it, "None of us is as smart as all of us."

Happily Ever After? Couplehood and Retirement

Hans and Barbara are hardly unusual. The spouse with the big career is used to driving everything while the spouse without the big career is used to accommodating everything. The inflection point of retirement offers the opportunity to reset things, even though we acknowledge that can be intimidating for both people. When working with one member of a marriage or life partnership, a twinge of intimidation can often be heard about how crossing the fault line between their present work and future calling will affect this core relationship. The shadow of the partner is never far behind. Which is why, in our two-day program, the first day is always exclusively with the retiring individual. We perform such deep work about who they are and what their life looks like when it's thriving that we don't want the dynamic with their partner to influence their honesty. Individuals will potentially withhold information or change their answers because they want this important "other half" in the room to be okay with what they say.

On day two, however, we always invite their spouse or partner. (Not that they always attend.) Sometimes our participants paint a picture of the relationship that mirrors this sentiment:

> My spouse and I live on very separate tracks, and it's going to stay that way. So I'll have to build this project on my own. And frankly, our marriage works because I'm gone most of the time. I need to figure out how to continue to be away from that house five days a week.

Knowing this, we proceed to design an accommodating plan for independent engagement.

But where there is a shared life, the nonretiring spouse is commonly a force to reckon with for the intense professionals who enlist our guidance. Let's say we're working with a sixtysomething man whose wife gave up her career early on to stay at home and raise the kids. (Often this was the only survival strategy for a family whose breadwinner worked marathon hours.) You can bet the husband's retirement causes his wife big anxiety. Her litany of jitters goes something like this: *Is he going to be okay? Where is he going to put all that energy he previously poured into his career? We're both used to having our personal space—will we start driving each other crazy?* Such concerns are understandable. We often joke with the nonretiring spouse: "We understand—you do not want or need a full-time supervisor following you around all day!" In an imagined dialogue with her spouse, she might say, *I've been running our lives for thirty years; stay out of my business!*

That said, many spouses are excited that their partners will finally be able to engage more with them, lend a hand when they need it, and finally relax on vacations. Those long-shelved projects and plans to travel together can now be put into action. The concerns tend to lie more in how daily life will look if their retiring spouse does not have engaging things to do that are separate and independent.

Often, the person who signs up for our program is just as solicitous about settling their partner's apprehensions as about getting themselves pointed straight. They're acutely aware that their spouse is concerned about the situation. To compound matters, the spouse at home generally doesn't know how to talk about it. They don't want to telegraph the sentiment of "I don't want you around." And yet they struggle to imagine what this new shared reality will actually be. "You're not a chill-out, hang-out-on-the-sofa person. So what are you going to be doing?" This mutual concern means our work must unfold in a stereophonic channel.

Thus, we ask both individuals to think expansively about the next decade of life. We pose a number of questions to each of them and then look for alignment and synergy. Often, it is instantly clear that there *is* a lot of alignment, and the funny thing is they're surprised by this insight! Most of the couples we've worked with have never had this conversation. It's not that they couldn't have done so; it's just that life is busy, and the daily grind of what needs to get done is what they talk about. This presents a rare opportunity to zoom out, look across the horizon together, and create an intentional vision of the life they'd like to build together from here.

When we think about how to construct a satisfying couplehood at this juncture in life, one very useful approach is to mock up a Venn diagram for each partner. Some want their Venn diagrams to overlap considerably. For others, the state of their union thrives on parallel play.

Me, You, We Venn Diagram

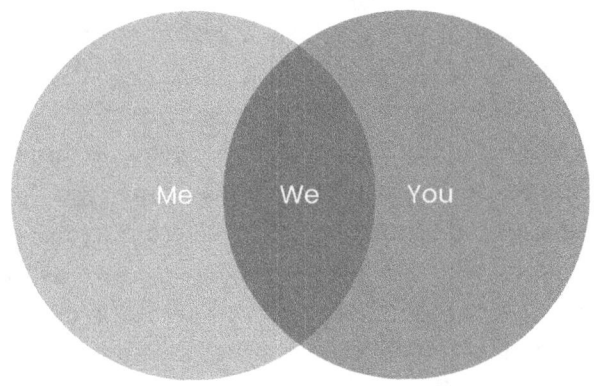

As we work with couples to get clear about their independent and shared opportunities, it goes something like this: "There's a set here that illustrates just your activities and a set there that illustrates just your significant other's activities. Neither of these sets intersects. But here is also an overlap where both of you enjoy moving in the same circles." We identify natural crossover like shared travel, interests, hobbies, or causes that both partners have been involved in and can now look forward to doing together.

A particularly resonant example of the benefits of joint planning is the dynamic duo of Kirk and Peggy Davenport, whom I introduced earlier. Here, we met a couple who pooled their skills to successfully reach goals collaboratively. These two individuals are not just roommates or co-parents. They are cocreators and partners in life. At the same time, each had to lay out their own independent goals.

As Peggy observed, "Kirk has a very strong gravitational pull. I love that, but it also scares me a little." She elaborated, "By retiring, I was letting go of my separate self in a lot of ways, so I had to make sure that I would not just become a planet orbiting Kirk's sun."

This potential asymmetry led Peggy to cordon off a space of her own. We affixed a big sheet of paper to the wall and dubbed it "Peggy's Sandbox." Later, we'd hear that metaphor for Peggy's independence worked its wonders long past our joint session. "I have to make sure I have my own sandbox," Peggy recalls reminding Kirk as they began building their new life together in Wyoming. She chuckled. "Best form of marriage counselling ever!"

As couples inventory their takeaways, there's no mistaking that sense of ease and delight they feel in possessing clear outlines for their togetherness. Both spouses invariably express great relief that they engaged in this shared planning opportunity: "Now there is a game plan. There is so much blue sky. We can see a future that contains each of us and both of us at the same time."

Where to Live: The High Stakes of Pulling Up Stakes

Peggy and Kirk Davenport also provide a dimensional case study of how couples successfully navigate the prospect of relocation. They confronted a big decision: whether to stay in New York City or heed the call of the wild. The quandary had loomed ever larger since 2013, when they finished building a vacation home on sixteen acres near Jackson Hole, Wyoming, teeming with elk, moose, and bears. It even graced the pages of the *Wall Street Journal*'s "Mansion" section. What's more, Kirk and Peggy had adult children who also loved the outdoors, and Kirk's stated goal was to ski one hundred days a year. For Kirk, Jackson Hole was a place he wanted to put down new rootstocks. He knew what the habitat offered, and the thought of retiring there quickened his pulse. Peggy loved it too—but only as a vacation place, not a permanent home. She recounts the clash of visions that loomed over their horizons:

> I was on board with the idea of leaving the firm while we were still very much in the game. And I was pretty open minded and curious about what a next chapter could look like. The conflict arose around the idea of moving to Wyoming. Kirk was the driver of that decision. That was extreme from my perspective. All my friends, my family, my community, values, and culture were in New York. I'm from outside of Boston, but I'm a little too expressive for New England. There was all the room in the world for my personality in New York, and I just loved all the different types of people I was around all the time. I thrived. Kirk felt there was another life he wanted to live. And that life was in Wyoming. I was like, "Yeah . . . we're going to need to talk about that!" Wyoming is not a very emotionally expressive place. It's not particularly culturally diverse. And it's on the flip side of New York City culture. Everything about it didn't seem obvious to me. So that was something we really had to work through.

Today, Peggy's views are suffused with the glow of self-fulfillment. The couple's original plan had been to relocate to Wyoming but to retain their New York apartment where they'd raised their kids, assuming they'd spend significant time there during the year. Ultimately, the only real estate they kept back East was a beach house on Long Island, where they've since spent every August; the two "shoulder seasons" take them to a condo they recently built in Mexico's Baja California. But during the remaining months, it's the Wyoming wilderness that has become home.

Peggy's instincts on the enormity of this decision were spot-on. Relocation is no small thing; it merits careful consideration and a runway for experimentation. We always tell people who are considering a move, "If you are relocating when you retire, you have a completely different project from someone who plans to stay put." The potential move itself becomes part of our session. You need to build a whole new community. You have to replace all your core services. You're pulling up your roots and starting over in far more exhaustive ways than if you remain where you are. Together, we drill down on the reasons someone believes they want to relocate and whether, in fact, it's what they truly want. If relocating absolutely feels like the right decision, we help our clients avoid one of the pitfalls people step into when they retire: namely, creating unintentional conditions for isolation. And the hangover effects of the recent pandemic have only heightened this risk.

Hidden Hazards

As more and more people left the workforce during the pandemic, a new catchphrase entered the lexicon: the Great Resignation. Yet some of those resignations were older workers who felt pressured to retire. So much so that the trend earned its own label: the Great Retirement. In the April 18, 2022, edition of the *Wall Street Journal*, Beth DeCarbo wrote a piece entitled "People Who Hate Retirement—and What the Rest of Us Can Learn from Them." She highlighted some of the hidden hazards of retiring to new locations. For example, people imagine they want to move to their vacation home. One retiree she featured who did just that left his fulfilling job at the University of Texas for his lakeside home in the Adirondacks. "After about a month there, he started questioning whether the place where he spent his summers is the same place where he wants to spend the rest of his life," the article reported. It quoted him as saying, "Culturally and intellectually, I'm lonely."[13] I well understood why.

And there's a host of other regrets I could imagine him and his wife expressing about having turned a rural retreat into the centerpiece of their lives. What serves a working individual when they need to get away from it all might not suffice on a full-time basis. There's possibly a dearth of diversity or activity in the more remote spot, to say nothing of the daily lifestyle that likely came with their former surroundings. And that's not counting the family, friends, colleagues, doctors, dentists, therapists, physical trainers, hairdressers, and whole heap of other relationships suddenly now worlds away. Sometimes moving is the right answer. Let's say you're already on the board of an organization there, or maybe you're an artist who's eager to be part of the local art scene, or perhaps one or more of your kids live in the area. Any of these reasons could make the move extremely rewarding. But sometimes moving is a mere fantasy. Therefore, drilling down on what's motivating the desire to move and what life will look like in this new habitat just makes sense.

We saw the challenges of this issue play out before our eyes as we worked with investment banker Martin and his wife, Cynthia, a successful author, who found what seemed to be the house of their dreams in sunny Scottsdale right in the middle of our sessions with them. Having spent many long years in Chicago, they were excited about starting a new life in a golf community. Martin would retire from his position with the bank in six months, and while Cynthia remained literary royalty, she could work her word magic from anywhere.

---

13   Wall Street Journal. "People Who Hate Retirement—and What the Rest of Us Can Learn from Them," April 18, 2022.

As it happened, David and I were there when the call came in from the Arizona realtor. More than that, we'd heard from Martin and Cynthia about the prospects of a move on the first day of our session. "One of the things we're thinking of is getting another house down here," Cynthia had explained. Martin intended to focus on his golf game. Beyond hitting the links, his big goal was "to get on the same page" as his wife. The grueling hours he'd sunk into his career had sapped time away from their marriage. Now he would have time to lavish attention on Cynthia's soaring career as an author, a side benefit of la dolce vita they both looked forward to.

So they lit out that afternoon and found the perfect property. At breakfast the next morning, Cynthia announced, "We found a house we love, and we put in an offer." As we sat down to lunch, her phone rang. "They accepted our offer!" she enthused. Under contract.

Be careful what you wish for. The transplants were soon to discover that the culture and attitudes of the insular golf community were not aligned with theirs. They felt painfully disconnected from what was important to them, struggling to find people of kindred interests and minds. The laid-back culture left them disoriented. There was a sameness to their days that, in contrast to the hubbub of Chicago, was a challenging adjustment. Another client who had parents in a retirement community there summed it up best: "The only way you know it's Sunday is the newspaper is thicker." Eventually, the couple realized their Arizona outpost would serve as a respite a few times a year when they weren't shuttling between Chicago and San Francisco, but it just wasn't the right place to call home.

Our concern from our session had been that a man with Martin's intellectual firepower would inevitably run out of juice in "leisure-ville." He did. However lovely playing golf and supporting Cynthia's work might have seemed in theory, in practice, it wasn't going to be enough. The moral of Martin and Cynthia's story? Relocating can seem like a splendid idea, but there's a lot involved in getting it right. Hard questions need to be asked and appropriate foundations laid.

In their fantasy of a more relaxed life, the couple didn't fully analyze whether it would provide cultural stimulation, social resonance, or even professional opportunity. For this reason, we often suggest that clients experiment with short-term leases in new locations before committing the time and money to fully relocating.

None of this is to say that relocating or shifting geography is a losing proposition. Not at all. Kirk and Peggy's happy transition proves otherwise. Rather, we emphasize that relocating on top of retiring is a monumental change that, in itself, deserves deep thought and intentional planning.

Often enough, moving is actually an imperative for our clients. A common theme is a desire to break ties with a tax-prohibitive jurisdiction. "We know we don't want to continue living where we are, but we don't know where we want to live." How to choose?

The compass might initially point in the direction of their adult children. Yet that needle starts to gyrate on closer consideration. Younger generations are more fluid in their thinking about career and geography, and they're not necessarily planning to put down roots in one place over several decades. As the parent, you say, *Huh, maybe we don't want to plan the rest of our days around the fact our oldest son happens to be living in North Carolina right now. We're the ones who have the freedom and the means to travel, so we can always travel to our kid*s. This realization tends to knock out all thoughts of following their offspring around.

So if the children aren't the deciding factor, what is? Any attempt to answer the "Where to?" question can only succeed as a cocreative exercise. Thus, on the day when a spouse joins us, we often roam the virtual globe. To launch the imaginative journey, we might say, "Tell us what would be true about the perfect place where you'd want to live." The trick is to stay nimble. "Let's not think about specific places," we counsel. "Rather, let's think about characteristics."

Here are some that came up in a recent exercise with a couple I'll call Daniel and Beth:

- "We want a small but sophisticated city." The first two corollaries to this ideal were "a great food scene and vibrant cultural attractions."
- Next on the list concerned the skies, as in: "The perfect place has more sun than gloom and a reasonably mild winter."
- Weather aside, it features "a political climate that is not at great odds with our values." Other musts included an advantageous tax rate, high-quality health care, and proximity to outdoor recreation spots.
- We also talked about lifelong learning opportunities, good air quality, and a low crime rate, as well as a low natural hazard risk.
- Last, but certainly not least, there had to be an international airport within an hour's drive.

There we were, conjuring utopia, when David asked, "Does it have to be in the United States?" The couple got very animated and gushed, "No! Actually, we've had some of our most enjoyable experiences in Europe. Why wouldn't we consider cities in Europe?"

Daniel quickly fired off a few cities they loved in Portugal and Spain. At this point, David suggested, "What you guys might want to do is identify all the international airports in southern Europe and draw the equivalent of a one-hour circle around them." Breaking into a duet of smiles, they explained that all their kids lived on the East Coast of the US, an easy plane ride from Europe's western shores. Hopping the Atlantic popped for them as a doable idea. The next step would be to test-drive the most promising spots for a few months apiece. And so, a plan emerged. Over the coming two years of city shopping, they took extended vacations whenever possible, both in the US and Europe. Their relocation project became as much about the adventure of discovering the right place as it was about ending up there. This outcome is a big part of what we do during our program: helping our clients break out of patterns of thought and habit that keep them limited. We fire up imaginations.

In our experience, as with all aspects of retiring, advance planning and a comfortable runway are even more important if relocation is on the agenda. Getting out in front of this potential change, cocreating the game plan, and leaving plenty of time for testing and reflecting are often the difference between a satisfying outcome and a disappointing and potentially costly one.

Parenthood and Retirement

Many of our clients and their life partners are undergoing another major change at the same time that retirement is looming. They have freshly finished raising their children. For these just-retired parents, especially full-time mothers, having their parenting duties reduced or nearly eliminated flips the trajectory of their lives and forces them to make fundamental adjustments. Virtually every moment of motherhood contains overwhelming love and joy, fear and pain, and everything in between. From being needed incessantly to needing to let go, the empty nester's release from intensity echoes the same inflection point as retiring from a career. Their purpose has changed, and their view of life has evolved. They must start organizing themselves differently with respect to time and energy while also making sense of it all.

Susan was a great example of a talented mother grappling with purpose and meaning as her children left the nest. She had opted to focus on the family while her husband, John, a successful accountant, focused on building his practice. As we worked with the couple, it became clear that John had a solid plan for his next engagement, having been invited by a family office client to act as a part-time CFO. We helped him validate the idea as an excellent fit for what he loved to do, and with some creative thinking, he could see the boundaries he'd place around the role so he protected time for other priorities in his life.

It was Susan who was struggling to define a satisfying future. Having mothered three children, the youngest of whom was starting college, Susan was facing her own "retirement" from motherhood. This is a common though little acknowledged theme for parents who have had the full-time child-rearing role. No one is throwing them a farewell party or buying them a gold watch as this chapter closes, and yet it feels like retirement all the same.

With Susan, we started where we always start: "Tell us about the moments when you have felt right on purpose—when you get that sensation that you are doing something you absolutely love." The answers came. Susan loved teaching. She loved cooking and developing recipes. She would demonstrate them on social media, often to great fanfare. Privately, she had studied thousands of pages of material about cooking and its importance to place and culture. She had much to say about the common language of food as a way to connect people across diverse cultures. And yet the tricky thing for Susan was the sense that she had no professional basis to believe in her abilities. She powerfully felt the absence of any external credential or validation of her knowledge and skill.

I countered, "What makes you a master at your craft is not a degree; it is the fact that you develop and test recipes. And who's to say you are not an expert in cooking? You've been doing it at a high level for decades." I urged her to forget the fact that she had not yet applied these talents professionally. "What would you do with these things if I could guarantee your total success?" I asked.

Susan's eyes widened as she leaned forward in her chair:

> I'd host a cooking show about cuisines all around the country. I'd research and write the episodes and design the dishes I'd cook for each one. I'd bring in cultural themes and look for ways to educate and enlighten my viewers about different parts of

the world. My goal would be to create connection through food.

This idea tumbled out of Susan's mouth almost fully formed. As we began to build this idea out more, Susan started to see that she had decades of material and thought invested already. With the abundance of platforms available to start sharing her content online, there was really nothing beyond her own mindset standing in the way of starting this project. A woman of enormous energy and determination, Susan was on her way.

Susan's example is an important reminder that the transition to empty nesting can be every bit as daunting as retiring from a demanding and lucrative career. In many ways, it is even harder because stay-at-home parents perceive an absence of third-party validation concerning their talents and accomplishments. And just like the retiring professional, the retiring parent is also navigating elements of loss and grief along with significant changes to identity and purpose.

Of course, not every couple shares the same circumstances when it comes to their children. Some couples still have younger children at home as retirement looms. Others have an adult child who, for a host of possible reasons, will need a lifetime of financial or other support. These factors affect finances, freedom, and peace of mind. While the interventions we can offer in such cases are necessarily circumscribed, we help people find resources that allow them to navigate critical next steps and build support systems that can evolve over time.

For example, we put clients in touch with niche wealth managers who can create special-needs trusts. Many—even most—of the tensions that seethe up in such cases center around a parent's day-to-day efforts to manage financial decisions for a dependent adult child. It can be psychologically challenging for parents to continue playing this role indefinitely. We recommend enlisting a dependable professional proxy who can handle both the finances and the fiduciary decisions for adult children with special needs. This allows the parents to go back to just being Mom and Dad instead of financial managers, boundary setters, or life planners. It's these roles that are exhausting for parents who are emotionally invested and can't easily make unbiased decisions for their adult kids. Similarly, caring for aging parents affects what's going to happen in this next period of your life. It helps to tap into a robust network of providers, examples of whom we readily share.

Designing the Off-Ramp

If imagining postcareer life is perplexing for many of our clients, designing the actual exit can be even more challenging, often conjuring an array of anxieties. These include becoming irrelevant too early, losing clients, having compensation cut, and somehow dropping out of favor with this all-important community of esteemed work relations.

For this reason, as much as David and I focus on helping clients build a plan for the future, we also prioritize shaping their exit strategy. While the specifics will vary depending on an individual's profession and organization, the common theme is a lot of sweaty conversations that most people would just as soon avoid. The reality is that a proactive approach, thoughtfully executed, is the key to getting this critical phase of working life right.

To use a sports analogy, games are won or lost in the fourth quarter. It can be an impressive performance right up to the final minutes, but the way it ends is the way it ends. Ensuring a strong strategy for succession is the best way to avoid defeat in the final plays of the career game. This does not mean we suggest going public with a retirement date too early; rather, the necessary work is to begin planning proactively so clients, peers, and younger colleagues are prepared for the future.

Let's start with the concern that clients will start heading for the door the moment a professional raises the idea of their future exit. Even if their retirement date is still years away, many worry that if they even mention the succession issue, what the clients will hear is "Oh you're going to be retiring soon, so we won't send work your way." In our experience, this is a fallacy. Succession planning is a core activity emphasized by enterprises of all types and sizes. As one large corporation put it to one of our law firm clients:

> Your team needs to be talking to us regularly about how you are developing the bench of lawyers who work on our matters. We want to know who is being groomed and who steps in for the leads if something happens to them.

In that and other clients' feedback, a distinct sentiment is encased. It says, in practical terms: we want to have regular dialogues about the future pipeline at your firm. A battery of questions and demands arises as a corollary of this imperative. Is the younger cohort working out for us? Is the current team adequate? Tell us about who's going to be in the lineup and ask us whether they meet our needs. And succession planning serves another high-priority agenda. Across corporate America, HR leaders are mindful of transformative trends in today's workforce. Creating, sustaining, and empowering diversity are all in step with this march of progress. In our experience, having frank discussions about succession is an avenue for deepening client relationships, not compromising them.

Perhaps even more crucial to a smooth and effective off-ramp is the willingness of a senior person to have transparent discussions within their own ranks. Hopefully, there is a cadre of younger talent coming up. When professionals are proactive about their succession, they are communicating to the next generation about the opportunities and responsibilities that lie ahead for them. For many younger professionals, it's critically important to understand that they have a path to opportunity where they are—that the senior partner today is not going to hang around for an extra ten years and destroy their chance at promotion or greater opportunity.

For this reason, internal succession planning can be a powerful talent-retention tool. For example, one of the most oft-cited reasons young partners leave law firms for competitors is that they don't see a significant opportunity for themselves. Typically, what precedes such a departure is the long muddle when a senior partner is either not planning to retire any time soon or not communicating their plan to retire. We've seen the wreckage that a lack of communication can bring about.

One senior partner, Charles, was so fearful of being frozen out of work that he stayed mum about his intention to retire the following year. His junior partner had no way of divining Charles's plan and took a position with a different firm, leaving Charles in the lurch. Suddenly, he found himself without a succession partner and had no recourse but to stay another three years. This unfortunate fate was entirely preventable with the merest discussion. It can take years to groom someone to take over a relationship with a particular client. That individual has to be integrated into the team and fully versed in the status of all aspects of the client's needs. You don't just flip a switch and drop in a new person.

Another version of the succession disaster occurs when an exiting partner grooms their inheritor but fails to notify the law firm in a timely manner. The domino effect that begins with the partner's silence interferes with the junior person's promotion opportunity. A conversation along the lines of "I need to train this person to take over my practice, and we need to get them into partnership soon" could have prevented a woeful chain reaction. Had that basic exchange taken place with the firm, the team, and the client, then all the working parties would have known what the plan was and how to communicate the right messages so the plan remained viable. Instead, what they got was, "Oh, we didn't know you needed her to step into your shoes in that time frame."

In short, we strongly advise our clients to start planning the shape of their off-ramp, ideally at least two years before they retire. We want them in the driver's seat. The point is to retire from a position of strength at the top of the game with all the necessary people and plans on board. The unappealing alternatives are a messy exit, lost clients, or, worse yet, a tap on the shoulder.

John brings to mind an example of overstaying one's welcome. After building and leading a core practice group at his firm for decades, the seventy-year-old partner was unceremoniously told his time was up. "The firm brought in a young partner to replace me without discussing it with me," he let out on a clear note of hurt.

> I was leading one of the most important client relationships, and with no discussion at all, they brought in my heir apparent. I've started to be sidelined and replaced, even though I am productive and busy. It's been disturbing to witness my own marginalization. I've been put on the bench.

John was still being paid though the end of the year, but he understood that he was now "irrelevant to the core work and the core client." To his horror, he felt like he was being quietly fired after what had been an illustrious career. And he was none too pleased.

John's story is not unusual. Rather than confronting the uncomfortable situation of retiring a long-active partner, many firms make decisions in ways that can't be ignored but are emotionally devastating. This is a clear instance in which the perceived taboo of even uttering the word *retirement* ended up hurting John. "It feels awful having all the power and relevance taken away from you," John said ruefully. "I've given everything to this firm." Indeed. Which is why we recommend taking control of the entire retirement process, including timing. Our advice? Leave on your terms with everyone wanting more.

Retiring to a Standing Ovation

Deciding when to retire is a multifaceted choice to be sure. However, the single most compelling principle to guide this decision should be how to leave on top. As I noted earlier, the way a thing ends has an outsize influence on one's view of the entire experience; ending a stellar career on a sour note is not just unfortunate—it is avoidable. Rather than be nudged or even pushed, it is possible to take control of when and how the finale plays out.

There are many factors that might drive one's decision to retire from an intense career. Every reason falls into one of two categories: it's either a push factor, or it's a pull factor. By a push factor, we mean forces associated with working life are operating to make the current situation less appealing. Perhaps the long hours and relentless demands are finally too much, or the work itself has lost its sparkle. Sometimes, culture at work has shifted over time, making it less of a fit for one's values. By a pull factor, we mean other interests or priorities are beckoning in a way that cannot be ignored. As one of our clients (a lover of adventure travel) put it: "At fifty-seven, I realistically have thirteen summers left to do the challenging trips I want to do; I've got to get on with it."

Push/Pull Factors Diagram
When to Retire

Push Factors		Pull Factors
Lack of Control		Freedom
Burnout		Travel
Changing Culture		New Purpose
Stagnation		Time with Friends & Family

When there is a combination of both push and pull factors, the decision to retire can feel more approachable. The tougher situation occurs when, although an individual still loves what they do and sees no reason to change course, their firm or employer has a different agenda. Many professions and industries are simply skewing younger as the decades go by, requiring people who imagined a limitless tenure to reassess their runway.

Whatever the situation, looking ahead in five-year increments is a helpful way to get out in front of timing to ensure that retirement remains firmly in control of the person retiring. Consider the trend at the office by asking one or all of these questions:

- Are colleagues retiring on the earlier side?
- What percentage of your peers are your age or older?
- What signals is leadership sending about when to retire?
- What are the push factors and pull factors in play?

The answers to these questions are specific to each individual, but they can help form the basis of a plan as to the timing and shape of the off-ramp. Taking a head-in-the-sand approach to these questions is almost never optimal or empowering.

By taking a proactive approach to when and how to retire, it is possible to define and execute on any important legacy projects that remain to be completed. Sometimes there are younger colleagues who need help with progression. The significant internal leadership role of a project might have a distinct term. By clarifying the specific years available before retirement, it is possible to make strategic decisions about what else can be accomplished or committed to.

Once an actual target date is chosen, the important question is when to go public with the decision. In our experience, going public about one's retirement date is like crossing the Rubicon. There is no going back, but it is also incredibly liberating as it opens up a world of possibility regarding future aspirations. (More on that in chapter 12.) For purposes of this discussion, it is enough to say that the announcement itself changes things for all involved. For colleagues, the reality of adjusting to a new working life sets in, requiring some to step into more responsibility and allowing others to embrace greater opportunity. If clients are part of the equation, they must begin to increasingly rely on others for assistance and expertise. The firm or company itself might revise some of its arrangements as well, including compensation. As I noted in chapter 3, these adjustments are a necessary part of constructing an effective and comfortable off-ramp that we refer to as the "taper."

The length of this taper period will necessarily differ from person to person, depending on their organization, profession, and other factors, but the idea is the same—to provide an adequate period of time to hand off responsibilities, adjust to the enormity of the coming change, begin working toward future endeavors, and create conditions that permit an empowered and intentional closure to a career. As for a fear of reduced compensation, which troubles many of our clients conceptually, we suggest really examining whether the brief period of reduced income will make any material difference to their financial prospects over the long run. If not, perhaps the more valuable exercise is to focus on creating a magnificent ending to the career, as opposed to fighting for the last dollar.

We counsel our clients not to miss out on two wonderful opportunities in this process—savoring and gratitude. By savoring, we mean paying close attention to certain meaningful events—the ultimate partners' meeting; the final holiday party; the last round of peer reviews; and those final, substantive, culminating moments of working life, like court hearings, client meetings, or deal closings. The recognition that these moments comprise the end of a tremendous life experience summons a level of attention and appreciation that can be truly significant and memorable.

Gratitude is another oft-overlooked but worthwhile opportunity. While most of our clients will be celebrated and lauded at the end of decades-long careers, they too have the chance to express deep appreciation to others for their efforts. To be sure, this applies to the peers and colleagues who have worked with them shoulder to shoulder, but we point out that it equally relevant to all the unsung heroes who are crucial to the operation of every enterprise—the assistants, administrators, and information technology team, for example. When clients proactively design ways to thank their colleagues, it often becomes a favorite part of their retirement. One client hosted a wine and cheese party at the office just for staff as a way to thank them for helping make his time at the firm so positive. Another reported that she brought an enormous food basket down to the IT team, announcing, "For once, I'm not here with a problem! Thanks to all of you for your incredible support of me over the years—even when I was ready to throw my computer out the window." As she put it to us later, "They were blown away that I would bother. That was, hands down, my favorite moment of the whole retirement project."

The goal is to design and execute on a positive finish to what has surely been an incredible career. Investing in the ending just makes sense. Given the choice, why not take your final bow to resounding applause?

Chapter Summary

Retiring is not a solo operation. Advance planning allows time for adequate coordination with the many people affected.

Many couples worry about how one spouse or partner's retirement will affect their relationship. Open discussions about the needs of each person are key to navigating this change, including not just how the couple's shared life will look but also how each person's independent life will look.

Relocation in retirement adds a host of additional challenges to this already-significant inflection point. Invest adequate time and investigation before committing to a new place, especially to find pathways that rebuild community.

As children are raised and become independent, the full-time parent might be facing their own loss of identity, purpose, and structure as they grapple with their version of retirement.

As much as planning for the future is key to a successful retirement, designing a strong professional off-ramp through proactive succession planning is also critical.

It is empowering to control the timing and experience of retiring by driving the decision and communicating it effectively. Part of retiring at the top means pacing the transition, savoring the meaningful moments, and expressing gratitude on the way out.

PART FOUR

MAKING IT REAL

Getting Started, Charting Progress,
and Enjoying the Ride

chapter ten

FROM OVERWHELM TO ACTION

I am rather like a mosquito in a nudist camp;
I know what I want to do, but I don't know where to begin.
~ Stephen Bayne, Episcopal leader

Where to Begin?

One of the great ironies presented to high achievers as they consider retirement is an unfamiliar disorientation. This feeling is caused in part by a previously unknown level of freedom (created by lots of time and just as much money) combined with a huge array of theoretical options for what to do next, most of which seem either too obvious or too outlandish. For perhaps the first time, there is no clear ladder to climb, no well-defined path stretching before them. And yet, there is an awareness of the abundance of resources they have—experience, skill, knowledge, wisdom, connections, financial security—an embarrassment of riches, one might say. But there is also a version of tunnel vision that nearly immobilizes the imagination.

In chapter 2, I alluded to this phenomenon of intellectual paralysis caused by too many choices. When we survey our clients at the start of our work, we ask what they want to get out of our time together. Invariably, the responses sound like this:

- I need to organize my thinking. I want to clarify my options and then map out a plan to explore them.
- I have some ideas, but I am not confident they make sense for me.
- I know I don't want to work as hard as I have been, but I can't think of anything that wouldn't require my full commitment.

All this brings us to the million-dollar question so difficult to answer when all the success boxes have been checked: What do you really want? That question can cause the most agile of minds to lock up. And for good reason, considering our clients have usually spent decades responding to what others want with lightning speed and impeccable competence. Stopping to ask what they want for themselves? Not part of the equation. "I've never even given myself permission to ask that question" is a common rejoinder. Part of our work is to ignite curiosity about what's out there that they haven't considered or explored.

So we get a little more specific with our inquiries. One of our favorites is "What do you want to *feel* more of in this next decade?"

We asked this question of Sarah, who had come to us weary of her current circumstances but with no clear sense of when or whether to retire. Three decades of her life had just gone toward a career in commercial litigation, and, at sixty, she'd muddled through for so long she felt fused with the haze: "I don't see any fresh challenges down the pike," she sighed. "I'm just kind of meh. I want to feel more alive."

No one was pushing Sarah out. Nor did she hate what she was doing. She simply felt like she had squeezed all the juice out of her career. On top of that, her kids had recently left home to begin their own journeys, opening up another chasm in her sense of purpose.

In recent years, Sarah would often wonder, *Is this really the best way for me to use my skills?* But a tug-of-war would then break out between her emotional and more practical inner whispers. *Then again, why would I leave at the peak of my career and earning ability?* She used to feel energized by the idea of billing more hours, thereby making more money, and her competitive nature would be fed by exceeding the annual quantitative targets set by her firm. Ultimately, however, she could no longer ignore the not-so-dull ache that nagged her, admitting, "I'm not energized by this anymore." She also wanted more flexibility in her Monday-to-Friday schedule. And, more stirringly, she coveted the gratification that would come from making a difference in the lives of individual people.

Like others in her wistful state, Sarah murmured of a thirst for renewal and exuberance but could not put her finger on how to get them. And yet, as we mined her nonwork activities for hidden treasure, we hit gold. The prior year, she had joined the board of an innovative private college, and they had just asked her to run its next capital campaign—both a compliment and an intriguing challenge. Her first instinct was to decline. "I have no time for that kind of commitment," she protested. Nevertheless, we asked her to paint a picture for us of what her ideal role might look like if she did accept the offer.

And there it was—the energy, the enthusiasm, the missing spark. We had already learned that Sarah excelled at developing powerful but nonobvious strategies—she did this in her legal cases all the time. Her other superpower was shaping messages that tell a coherent and persuasive story. When we dug into some of her more personal interests, she revealed that she loved putting together enriching events for others, although this had never found a relevant home in her professional life. It was suddenly apparent to Sarah how she could weave these aspects of herself together in a fresh way, and the capital campaign could be the perfect context.

As Sarah looked ahead at her possible involvement with the school, she could envision leading it into a realm of added significance by making attendance more economically accessible. Her voice hit bright notes as she continued:

> We wouldn't limit the number of financially challenged students we let in. The long-term vision would be to build an endowment and make attendance accessible through scholarships. If I do that, I will feel like I have done something that matters.

Just the wisp of this vision was enough to visibly energize Sarah, and she could already see some new strategic approaches to the school's future capital campaign centered around this objective. With a plan to retire from law in two years now coming together, Sarah had a new pathway to build toward—one that felt like a healthy stretch but was also grounded in her strengths and interests.

Sarah's story provides an instructive example about where to start. "Right where you are, with exactly what you have" is how we put it. But the key is to expand the mind and fire up the imagination. Enter brainstorming and lateral thinking.

Generating Ideas: The Art of Brainstorming

American scientist and author Linus Pauling is noted for observing that "the best way to get a good idea is to get lots of ideas." I could not agree more. For this reason, we use expansive brainstorming exercises to identify potential pathways for staying engaged and relevant after an intense career.

We've all heard the word *brainstorming*, but its origin and definition are instructive. The term was originally coined by Alex F. Osborn in his 1953 book *Applied Imagination: Principles and Procedures of Creative Thinking*. Since then, the term has become widely recognized throughout the world. According to *Merriam-Webster*, brainstorming is defined as "a group problem-solving technique that involves the spontaneous contribution of ideas from all members of the group; the mulling over of ideas by one or more individuals in an attempt to devise or find a solution to a problem."[14] Brainstorming has become synonymous with the creative process of generating ideas, but to be effective, the process requires adhering to some important guidelines, as the text box on page 184 summarizes. Among two of the most important of these are the generation of many ideas and the deferral of judgment on those ideas until later. Neither of these rules is particularly easy for our high-competence clients who are strong analytical thinkers and quick to spot potential flaws.

As we set the stage for this exercise, we emphasize a single criterion for an idea to land on our brainstorming list: Is it interesting enough that it warrants further investigation? The goal is to generate lots of ideas, expanding the realm of what's possible. As Osborn so perfectly put it, "It is easier to tone down a wild idea than to think up a new one."

Similarly, while we are brainstorming, we ask that everyone in the room suspend the "Yes, but . . ." chorus that so often jumps to mind—notably when an idea most excites a client. It's a lucky moment when the body and psyche speak in harmony. I'm thinking of that auspicious crossing when a client both vocalizes excitement and becomes wistful. In such instances, we'll make a note that we just might have hit on a closely held dream.

Yet for some individuals, the stakes are so high emotionally that the safer course is to squelch the idea before they fall in love with it. Before we even begin to explore execution, I can see that critical mind jump in and douse the flame of excitement. *Come on, it's never going to happen.* This is the inner cynic trolling—and we ask that inner cynic to sit patiently aside until we finish brainstorming.

---

[14] "brainstorming," Merriam-Webster.com, 2011, https://www.merriam-webster.com, accessed January 14, 2024.

Ten Guidelines for Effective Brainstorming

Create a Positive Environment: Choose a comfortable and open space and insist on a positive and nonjudgmental atmosphere where participants feel free to express their ideas.

Define the Problem or Goal Clearly: This helps focus everyone's thinking.

Set a Time Limit: A defined time period encourages rapid mental activity and prevents overthinking.

Encourage Quantity over Quality: Emphasize the generation of a large number of ideas without evaluating them initially. The focus is on quantity, not quality, at this stage.

Build on Others' Ideas: Bring a collaborative mindset to build on or modify the ideas of others.

Defer Judgment: Discourage immediate criticism or evaluation of ideas during the brainstorming phase. Save judgment for a later stage to avoid stifling creativity.

Use Diverse Techniques: Employ various brainstorming techniques, such as mind mapping and lateral thinking (see below) to stimulate fresh ideas and connections.

Combine and Refine Ideas: After the initial idea generation phase, review and combine similar or related ideas. Refine and organize them to create a more structured set of potential solutions.

Evaluate and Prioritize: Once a diverse set of ideas is generated, evaluate and prioritize them based on relevance, feasibility, and potential impact.

Take Action: Develop an action plan based on the prioritized ideas. Assign tasks, set deadlines, and implement the chosen solutions.

During any brainstorming exercise, we recommend bringing at least one other person into the conversation with you. Ideally, the session should involve two to four people in a room together where you're relaxed, there's no time pressure, and you bring a sense of fun. It should feel very low stakes because it can't go wrong. You are just generating ideas, after all, not making commitments.

Get things rolling by having someone (other than you) ask, "What are all the things you like to read about? What topics do you find absorbing?" It's fun. It's almost like a game, as in, "How much stuff can we put on this sticky note?" Then you can have your partner or group member move on and ask another pointed question, capturing the responses. In our client brainstorming sessions, we like to use giant sticky notes and slap those up on the wall to create "mind maps," which are incredibly useful.

A mind map is a visual depiction of a lot of connected material. It's not linear, like a list. There is a central circle that identifies the subject of the brainstorm: perhaps "industries." And on one spoke moving out from that center could be various industries that are intriguing, such as "adventure travel," "wine," and so on. It becomes a diagram. The science shows that mind maps extend our cognitive ability to hold all this disparate material together at the same time so we can make meaningful and creative connections. If we try to do the same thing with a vertical list of words, connections do not appear as readily.

Mind Map Example (#1)

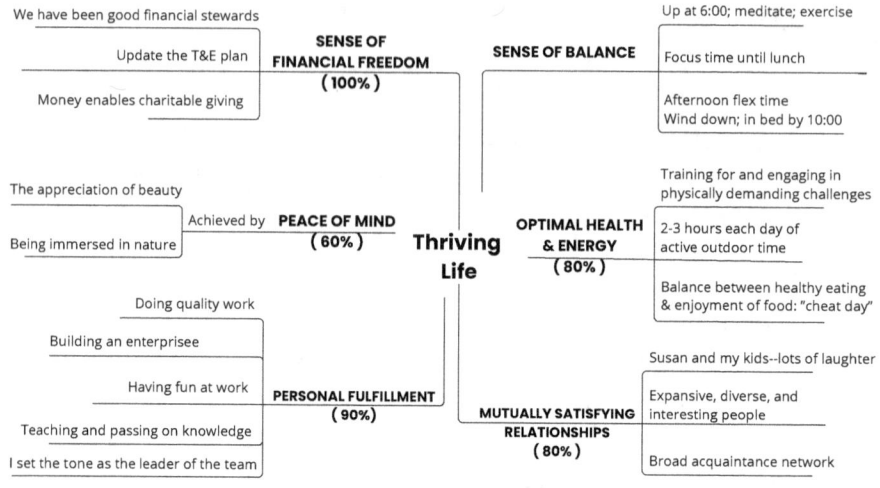

Mind Map Example (#2)

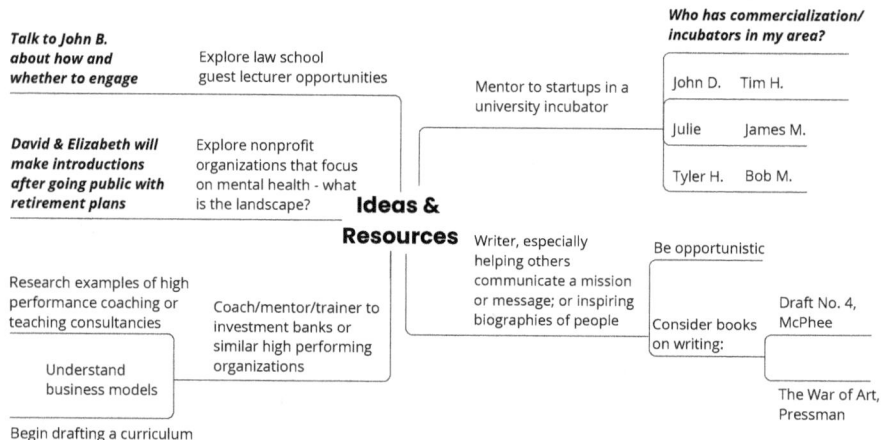

As part of our brainstorming technique, we also employ aspects of lateral thinking to boost creative output. *Lateral thinking* is a term coined by Maltese physician and creativity expert Dr. Edward de Bono in the late 1960s. It refers to a thinking style that involves approaching problems and generating solutions from unconventional and unexpected angles. Unlike vertical thinking, which follows a logical and linear path to solve problems, lateral thinking encourages the exploration of diverse ideas and possibilities.

Our application of the lateral thinking concept involves separately brainstorming several different categories of information and then looking for connections that spark ideas. Questions might include:

- What are the things you love to do?
- What issues do you care about?
- What topics do you find yourself gravitating toward in your reading?
- What are the activities and who are the kinds of people you find most absorbing?
- What specific industries or organizations seem to capture your attention?

To enable the freest thinking, we stress that there need be no intention to formally engage with any topic or area—we just want to inventory a wide range of intriguing subjects.

Then we move on to making a list of organizations a client is curious about as well as the attributes of organizations that are a good fit. For example:

- Do you enjoy working with grassroots organizations just forming, or is that too new for you?
- Is there anything about the size or geography of an organization that grabs you?
- What are the organizations that have caught your eye or that you want to know more about?

Having populated the first two lists, we move on to potential roles. When we drill down on preferred methods of engagement, we might hear things like "I'm a terrific writer"; "I can sell ideas"; "I can recruit people"; "I'm a great teacher"; "I'm a great board member." We will also explore questions such as "Do you prefer to generate big ideas and delegate execution, or do you enjoy advancing or refining the big ideas others have?"

Another profitable line of inquiry concerns the audiences our client would most like to benefit. Are these young people? Are they disrupters? The elderly? Women who are trying to succeed in the professional realm? Or perhaps disadvantaged groups or individuals who are seeking to improve their circumstances?

As these independent lists take shape, we start to look for connections. It is then that we see some of the liveliest and most personally intriguing ideas jump out. Bob Wyman's story immediately comes to mind.

Bob grew up exploring nature in New England and Kentucky in the fifties and sixties. During those years, the great outdoors was coming under increasing assault from contamination caused by industrialization and urbanization. A growing chorus of advocates felt that Earth's land, water, and air should not be left to fend for themselves. By the time Bob joined his law firm in 1981, environmental law was an emerging field. With the support of his firm, the crusading lawyer developed and helped oversee its global environmental department from 1988 until his 2020 retirement.

With retirement in the wind, he enlisted our input in September 2018. While Bob was looking at his future with optimism, he wanted to ensure he did not miss a meaningful opportunity for his next chapter. And this is where brainstorming can be so helpful.

Bob was known for inventing unique solutions to big intractable problems in the environmental space. Some of the biggest strides in regulating greenhouse gasses had come from incentives he devised in carbon emissions trading. A keystone of his practice was helping clients in numerous industries manage energy-related risks proactively. Lobbying Congress in the late eighties, he brought his economic training and lawyerly deliberation to bear on its amendments to the

Clean Air Act. That states could now regulate industry with greater use of economic instruments marked one of Bob's proudest achievements. "The concept of putting a price on pollution made a lot of sense to me because it encouraged pollution reduction, rewarded innovation, and provided flexibility for parties who had trouble complying in a specific way," Bob recounted.

History also came alive in his reflections on helping the Environmental Protection Agency craft regulations that enabled the private sector to monetize new technologies. And that same sense of gratification remained vivid in the way he talked about his early nineties stint designing the Southern California Cap-and-Trade Program with a coalition of twenty-five companies:

> This was the first urban, multi-pollutant and multi-industry Cap-and-Trade Program in the world. It was a lot of fun. I spent thousands of hours doing it. My dad was an engineer, so I grew up comfortable with manufacturing and believing it was the heart of an economy. I was able to marry my support of the economy and the manufacturing sector with my love of the environment, recognizing that, as miraculous as manufacturing and energy were for a hundred years in fueling our quality of life, they also had a dark side that we were learning about, which was their impact on the planet. A lot of my career as a public policy advocate was about balancing these factors. It was very personally rewarding.

Coming up with unique ways to shape human behavior rather than merely regulate it with statutes was Bob's long suit. On the brink of retirement, he believed he wasn't finished influencing the way people think about climate change. He described a core issue hampering effective communication in this space: "We have a messaging problem with climate change," he stressed. Discussions about the causes of climate change polarize people while discussions of consequences often paralyze them. But people can get excited about technology solutions, particularly if they can experience them in a multisensory way. He had seen the shortfalls of merely telling people what not to do and felt one of the critical ingredients of a behavioral pivot was sensory engagement. According to Bob, hope lay in bringing participants into immersive experiences to discover current climate impacts today and what they will look like over the next fifty years.

As we brainstormed with Bob about his world of ideas, interests, and unique capabilities, themes emerged. Climate change was high on the list of ideas that intrigued him. He spoke about the fact that he liked designing and launching bold initiatives and was not daunted by start-up entrepreneurship. And he wanted to change the way the world was headed. With all this in mind, we helped him put shape to a new nonprofit he would ultimately create.

Before we knew it, Earthshot was born. Its formal mission is "inspiring climate action by engaging people in activities that immerse them in a positive empowering cleantech message." Otherwise put, the organization produces augmented, virtual, and real-life experiences and stories to make the science of climate change accessible and interesting. People of all ages and backgrounds can interact with a multimedia installation at a venue or with a video game online and understand on a sensory level what is happening and why it matters. Leaving policy and theory behind, the creative challenges aim to spark wonderment and a desire to join together in making a positive impact.

For Bob, Earthshot has been the ideal way to create a lasting legacy while tying up his working life in a coherent way. His professional contribution seemed incomplete until he was able to think about how to bring together his unique genius, his expertise, and his relationships to create something with lasting impact. What began as an amorphous idea, once shaped and defined, seemed to manifest almost overnight. Earthshot launched in the summer of 2019, less than a year after our session, and continues to pursue innovative and impressive climate change initiatives to this day. And for Bob, it is a perfect expression of author Frederick Buechner's eloquent maxim: "You find your vocation at the spot where your deep gladness meets the world's deep need."

But how did Bob move this inspiring idea from paper to reality? In part, he employed the two most powerful questions we know to move from any new idea into purposeful action: What else do I need to know? and Who can help? The initial steps required to begin nearly anything flow out of these questions.

What Else Do I Need to Know?

It's fun to come up with big ideas like Earthshot, but a plan for implementation is what brings them to life. A cornerstone of our approach is to facilitate this process by helping our clients create an approachable action plan.

The first question, *What else do I need to know?* clarifies the sort of research required before an idea can be properly defined. Using this question, we build a to-do list for information gathering that preempts the threat of inertia. After all, our clients are crackerjack researchers, regardless of the topic.

For its instructive value, here is an example of an often-intriguing idea and a research road map that could serve as a starting point for someone wanting to pursue it. Many of our clients are experienced in business matters, whether they are lawyers, accountants, investment bankers, or executives. We also often hear that, along with their core professional duties, mentoring younger people has been one of the most satisfying aspects of working life—one they will miss. Nearly every client also expresses a desire to find new collaborators and communities with whom they can connect and share interests.

With this palette of desires, we might suggest to a client the possibility of mentoring start-up companies that are attached to university incubators. Most of our clients simply don't know this option exists. When they hear about it, they're duly intrigued. It represents a mix of innovation and fledgling companies, usually led by young people who need guidance and the wisdom of experience. There's the added attraction of flexibility. As a volunteer, the mentor-in-residence for a university incubator can build flexibility into the arrangement and essentially control their schedule. And as is true for the vast majority of our clients, they do not need current pay for their efforts—a perfect fit for cash-starved start-ups (although an equity stake is not out of the question).

Having lit the fuse of interest, we will ask our client what else they need to know to rule this idea in or out as a viable option for them. The resulting research checklist might look something like this:

- What colleges and universities are in my area?
- Which of them have incubators or other entrepreneurial support programs?
- Which of those incubators or programs use mentors?
- Who runs those programs, and how would I contact them?
- What sorts of start-up companies are working with these programs?
- What other needs do these incubator programs have?
- Are there any associations that link these kinds of organizations together?

Running down the answers to the above questions provides an immediate and approachable avenue for action. More often than not, our clients deploy research experts to assist them in their quest, including the knowledge management teams in their firms or organizations. As information is gathered, more definition comes. More often than not, our highly connected clients discover they know someone who knows someone who can help. This takes us, then, to our other favorite question for getting into action.

Who Can Help?

This question so energized Bob Wyman that before he knew it, he was drafting a live business plan. The bones of the endeavor were formed right there in the room with us and inspired a host of strategies to drape over them. He conceived the idea of approaching curators at museum venues and quickly got traction. He reached out to his law firm colleagues for advice and connections. Piece after strategic piece fell into place as he amassed a board of eighteen absolute luminaries in relevant fields.

While the labor of getting Earthshot off the ground was plenty intensive, Bob's work hours going forward would not be. It was important to him to make sure he did not take on another monolithic job. He set Earthshot up with the right economic support and people so it didn't fall entirely on his shoulders. Some of the financing came from his fundraising efforts in his law firm, as well as others outside his firm. And he was gratified when Earthshot, by virtue of its mission, qualified for pro bono support from his colleagues.

> The week after our session, I sent an email around to people in the firm who were keyed in to the topic of climate change. It was just a "Little Red Hen" request saying, "Anyone interested in working with me?" Being the wonderful institution it is, I got about fifty responses. Whatever their reasons, I was so gratified that so many at the firm wanted to help me build Earthshot. We incorporated it and created a nonprofit before I retired.

The nearly seventeen months between our session and Bob's last day at the firm dovetailed nicely with the demands of birthing a new venture. This ample lead time "proved to be a good thing since it took a while," he reflected. In his quest to build a viable project, he also looked beyond the perimeter of his firm, but his presence on the firm platform was undoubtedly helpful as he sought to expand the universe of his collaborators. Here, he retraces key tactical steps of his outreach:

> I contacted someone whom I knew from the academic community when I was briefly on a climate change strategy team for University of Southern California. He had been the director of USC's Energy Institute, and I had also worked with him as a consultant for companies in the start-up space doing all sorts of things, from building electrical airplanes, to reengineering waste (so you don't need landfills anymore), to using waste to create jet fuel. He'd worked in the Clinton administration in the Office of Science and Technology Policy, and I knew he was someone with whom I could work well, as we had, and who knew the energy transition space quite well. So I approached him and asked, "Would you be interested in doing this with me?" And he said, "I can think of nothing I'd like better." Since I couldn't be my own client while I was still at the firm, I couldn't be the CEO of this entity. So I became a board member and chair of the board. We left it at that, and it's worked well.

Asked about any advice he'd share with others who want to do something meaningful in retirement, Bob muses:

> Find the people in your life who stimulate your thinking, and whom you can help, and then spend time with them. And if there are other people out there who you think could play that role in your life, take the initiative to connect with them.

Bob is living proof you can start leveraging your relationships and areas of expertise in a meaningful way while you're still employed, and you can continue after you've left. He's also a shining example of someone who has created a legacy that feels fully purposeful. It helps solve that all-important agency question of *How do I stay relevant and connected and continue to use my skills in a meaningful way?*

Bob has created a platform for himself that provides continued engagement, connection, community, and meaning. He had a wonderfully optimistic sense of how he could devise fresh and interesting ways to experience the sustainment his firm had given him. The arc of his story is an excellent reflection of his skills and passions. A lot of his former partners are watching him and saying, "Wow!"

When I tell him this, he says:

> The truth is a lot of my former partners are helping me! Their commitment to pro bono work is really quite meaningful, and we could not be doing Earthshot without the input and support of some very smart and skilled lawyers at the firm.

The Power of Your Network

I absolutely love this observation by entrepreneur and author Ben Casnocha:

> Opportunities do not float like clouds in the sky. They're attached to people. If you're looking for an opportunity . . . you're really looking for a person.

Whatever any of us is trying to create, find, build, or otherwise manifest, it will almost certainly involve, if not require, other people. For this reason, we urge our clients not to overlook the incredible opportunities and resources hidden in their extensive network of relationships.

With some frequency, we guide individuals who, though retiring from their current careers, are not ready to hang up their spurs; instead, they see another five-year-plus run ahead of themselves and want to secure another significant role. Their minds turn first to job boards and headhunters, but we strongly urge them to moderate those approaches in favor of a systematic networking strategy. By the time retirement from a major career is upon them, rarely will any posted position be a fit. Rather, we find that our clients end up *creating* the bespoke roles they desire for themselves by defining them clearly and then finding the person or organization who needs them, even if that person or organization did not previously know it.

This very situation came up for Edward "Ted" Sonnenschein, who came to work with us in 2019, two years ahead of his planned retirement date. He had spent more than forty years representing public and private companies and private equity firms in high-stakes mergers and acquisitions, joint ventures, restructurings, and spin-offs, as well as holding numerous leadership positions at his law firm. Ted didn't know precisely what sort of work he wanted after retiring from the firm, only that he wanted to keep working and that his advisory work was still fulfilling to him.

In a broader sense, Ted was clear about the strengths he longed to build on in his next endeavor. Chief among these were his ability "to provide guidance and judgment" as well as his "capacity to understand a vast amount of detail and complexity and then to distill and explain it to others," he said. His track record of "creating order out of chaos in a deal context" remained a point of pride for Ted as well. He stressed his satisfaction with the accomplishments of his law career and made no bones about wishing to remain employed, even if not full time.

"I set about trying to find a role for myself as a sixty-seven-year-old lawyer, which was probably not going to be a traditional in-house role," Ted recalls of his jumping off point. "I started looking for less conventional settings such as family offices," he adds, noting that our directions helped him chart his navigational course. "Talk to everybody you know who is involved in the business world," we had said. "Let them know what you're looking for. Get their advice and ask who else you should be talking to."

Ted combined an explorer's intent with the wisdom of "If not now, then when?" as he went about finding his North Star. We savored his report:

> Ultimately, your networking instructions landed me in a conversation with an investment banker I'd known since we were both very junior and with whom I'd had interactions on and off through the years. I'm a natural introvert who can make himself extroverted when he needs to be. That's how I developed business. But unlike business development, which is quite targeted, this experience was not a straight line. It was just an expansive approach of *Talk to everybody you know.* Some were people I hadn't talked to in fifteen or twenty years.
>
> Every one of them was receptive. For example, a person I hadn't been closely in touch with in about thirty years was extremely welcoming. He was a college classmate with whom I'd been in one business situation as well as a college fundraising event and one or two social situations. Though he was based in Los Angeles, he introduced me right away to someone in New York who took me to lunch and gave me great advice. Other business leaders whom I had last seen many years earlier or was just introduced to by another contact were also extremely generous with their time and advice. I was getting enough positive reinforcement that I decided networking was very satisfying. I began to get into a groove.

Ted's commitment to his networking strategy paid off. He started his new role in the summer of 2021, the day after he retired. That's when he became strategic adviser (he's now vice chairman) of an innovation and investment firm and family office that builds companies focused on space, technology, and energy. Ted didn't just sit around and expect ripened fruit to fall by his side. He executed on the networking and action plan we devised in our session with him, to great effect and success. And he followed our advice to propose a trial period of ninety days—an easy yes for his new employer and a safe experiment for Ted.

> When I got to my current opportunity, I wasn't sure it was exactly the right thing. It has a family office component to it, but it's not really a traditional family office. At the time, I was getting some traction with traditional multibillion-dollar family offices. Then, thanks to a combination of encouragement from you, David, and my wife, and my own instincts, I said, "Let's give this a try." So the founder and I set up a trial of a few months. It just clicked, and we both decided it was going to work long term.

Today, Ted is happily engaged in his new role. Here's a typical expression of his joy at having seamlessly parlayed his skill set as he describes his role in some recent transactions involving the company:

> We've recently had two very large deals requiring an intellectual capacity to centralize, integrate, and distill detail and then decide what to prioritize. In this job, I've been able to apply those skills to giving advice and making decisions well beyond purely legal matters.

Ted's story highlights an important social network theory introduced by sociologist Mark Granovetter in his seminal 1973 paper titled *The Strength of Weak Ties*. The theory challenges the conventional wisdom that strong ties (our close relationships) are the most valuable connections in social networks. Instead, Granovetter argues that weak ties (our casual or peripheral acquaintances) can provide unique advantages in accessing diverse information, opportunities, and resources.

Granovetter's theory emerged in the context of understanding how individuals find employment. Traditionally, it was believed that strong ties, such as close friends and family, were the primary sources of job information. Granovetter's empirical finding indicated that a significant proportion of job seekers learned about job openings through weak ties, like the friends of friends or the colleagues of friends, rather than strong ties. The resulting theory posits that our weak ties bridge different social groups, allowing for the exchange of novel information and opportunities. It is through engaging with our weak ties, thereby intentionally moving into new social and professional ecosystems of human beings, that exponential effects happen. In contrast, strong ties tend to move in the same social circles and share similar information, limiting exposure to diverse resources.

Because our weak ties act as channels into new social networks, they also provide access to nonredundant information that may be unavailable within our close-knit circle, suggesting that weak ties are especially valuable in connection with entrepreneurship, innovation, and the spread of ideas. In other words, if you never put yourself outside of your close circle of five friends, you will never hear anything new. You already know most of what they know!

Some Benefits of Our Weak Ties

Diversity of Information: Weak ties facilitate the flow of diverse information that might not be present in one's immediate social circle.

Access to Resources: Weak ties provide access to resources and opportunities not known by our strong ties.

Innovation and Entrepreneurship: Weak ties offer new pathways to innovation and entrepreneurship as diverse connections foster creativity and the exchange of novel ideas.

With weak ties in mind, we offer a simple but extremely effective formula for networking that is grounded in two strategic objectives: seek advice and seek introductions. We suggest creating an inventory of the three to five people who are most knowledgeable about or connected to the goal a client has and then setting up meetings with these objectives in mind. The framework is straightforward: "Here is what I am setting out to do—what advice do you have for me?" A wealth of information and feedback can come out of this simple question.

The follow-on inquiry is "Whom else should I be talking to?" This question leads to warm introductions to new people (weak ties) that often open the crucial door, as in Ted's case, to just the person our client needs to find. We never cease to be amazed at the results that flow from this process when followed faithfully and systematically. Please note here the most important conversations you will have will happen in person. It's particularly important to highlight this fact after the recent pandemic because we've all gotten comfortable interacting via a screen. While that can be a good option for nonlocal contacts, don't miss the opportunity, when you can, to actually take someone to lunch. The three-dimensional energy you'll have with someone is much more powerful and memorable than a phone call, email, or Zoom session.

Tracking Networking Efforts Template

Priority	Name	Company & Position	Email & Phone	Meeting	Location & Time	Status	Notes

Remember Who You Are

When we propose our tactical advice for getting into action, we often see a mix of exhilaration and fear. After all, as I highlighted in chapter 3, we are urging our clients out of the safety of their comfort zones. But we remind them that everything they still want is waiting for them beyond their comfort zones, so the uncomfortable stretch is part of the deal. Confronted with the unknown and unfamiliar, sensations of self-doubt and vulnerability leap to the fore. Part of our job is to transform those sensations from anxiety to enthusiasm.

It is in part for this reason that we delve into our clients' career origin stories—how they started down their professional paths, the mix of luck and hard work that landed them key opportunities, and the resilience they developed as adversity reared its head over the years. Our clients have incredible grit, but they are so used to their grittiness they forget it's there at all. We ask them to tell us about a memorable setback along the way and how they recovered. Stories abound with themes of endurance, hard work, force of will, self-confidence, and commitment.

In reconnecting with these stories, not only do our clients remember who they are and what they're made of, but they also educate us about their ability to manifest outcomes that have, quite frankly, already eclipsed their wildest expectations for themselves. "When you started out, did you ever imagine you'd be operating at this level one day?" Without fail, we see a moment of deep appreciation for themselves, their accomplishments, and the sheer determination it took to stay on the course they plotted, regardless of setbacks or self-doubt. "Remember who you are," we tell them.

Another of our favorite exercises for activating the natural determination in our clients is to pose this thought experiment: "How would you tackle this project if a client asked you to figure it out? Forget for a moment that you are acting on your own behalf—how would you get this done for someone else?" With this single shift of the mind, strategies and tactics begin tumbling forth, which we translate into an energizing action plan. Somehow, the idea that we are acting for our self-interest squelches the creativity that lives inside us for the benefit of others.

And of course, there is the opportunity to connect with the sense of a new beginning, not just the end of a career. As I noted in chapter 2, we treat retirement like a kind of graduation, where all the accumulated knowledge, experience, relationships, and wisdom are now available to apply in new and expansive ways. "Of course, your mastery of the previous challenges has been fulfilling and validating," we say, "but surely, you are not done evolving, learning, and exploring, are you?"

Aikido instructor George Leonard puts it perfectly: "How long will it take me to master aikido?" a prospective student asks. "How long do you expect to live?" is the only respectable response. Onward.

Chapter Summary

A combination of newfound freedom and lingering tunnel vision can make it difficult to organize and evaluate options for future engagement.

Brainstorming and lateral thinking can be effective tools for firing up the imagination and generating lots of ideas, which can later be sorted and prioritized.

Every good idea can be explored through targeted research and focused conversations with knowledgeable people, who can open new and profitable doors to more conversations.

Our networks are among the most powerful assets we have for lighting up pathways to new opportunities, especially our "weak ties" (or second-degree connections) within those networks.

Reconnecting with our many hard-won accomplishments, our vanquished setbacks, and evidence of our grit can supercharge the confidence we need to push out of our comfort zones in pursuit of the next challenge.

chapter eleven

STAYING IN THE BOAT AND ENJOYING THE RIDE

Let success mean only that you're committed,
and failure only that you've made insufficient progress.

~ Alex Lickerman, MD, author

I'd like to share a story here that proves helpful to our clients as they embark on new and sometimes unnerving adventures. In the summer of 2015, I stood with my family on the brink of what now seemed like a somewhat ill-conceived idea, given the ample opportunities for disaster. As part of a vacation in Santa Fe, New Mexico, we signed our family up for a whitewater rafting trip down the Rio Grande River. This had all sounded quite thrilling several weeks earlier when it was nothing but theory and a hazy projection of an exciting but altogether safe undertaking. Now our guide had gathered us around to review the numerous ways in which we could actually die having this completely voluntary experience. My mind took to catastrophizing almost right away as I tugged on my husband's sleeve and murmured, "Are you sure this is a good idea?"

Things only got worse when the lawyer in me read over the lengthy waiver typed in eight-point font, reminding me yet again— in writing, no less—that the river was a mighty force that could not be predicted or controlled with certainty, and I was knowingly casting myself and my family into a certain amount of existential risk. *You agree that our company will not be held responsible for death or bodily injury.* Oh boy.

With a menacing doom loop scrolling in my head, I surveyed David and our four teenaged kids as they anticipated the sheer magnificence of the experience awaiting us. They exuded the enthusiasm and elation that comes with embracing something new and a little bit risky. They seemed to trust the relative safety of the situation more than they feared its uncertainty. Our guide appeared to be deeply competent. Thousands, if not millions, of others had navigated this rambunctious river before us. We had a high-quality raft, life vests, and lots of safety instructions.

It was then that it hit me: what we came for was a ride on the river. Sure, the safer thing would be for us to hop back on the bus, drive several miles down the hill, and then put our raft into the river five hundred feet from the end of the trip. But what would be the point of that? Every memory we were about to make together required us to actually ride the river. Was I going to allow my mental projections of calamity rob me of the lived experience I came here to have? Deep breath. No, I was not. I wanted a ride on the river.

And with that, I signed my name to the waiver and forged ahead. Our ride that day was indeed, at moments, terrifying, but it was also altogether magnificent and exhilarating.

The point of this story is not to impose my personal risk tolerances on anyone else. But it does serve to remind our clients that they signed up to work with us because they wanted another "ride on the river." If comfort and safety were their only objectives in retirement, there would be no need for our help. Part of our job, then, is to help breathe life into their big ideas, especially when they seem most out of reach.

Don't Kill the Dream

David Shapiro's postretirement chapter provides one of the best examples I have of someone with a big dream who easily could have killed it flat but instead gave it a chance. His story is one we share with clients routinely because it is nothing short of inspirational.

David came to us in 2016, one year before his curtain call at his law firm. Professionally, he was a real estate lawyer, but it was clear he had a true love for the performing arts. During the first day and a half of our sessions, theater came up repeatedly as he explained he did have some involvement, though only on the periphery as a consumer, investor, and nonprofit board member. Other ideas he expressed enthusiasm for included travel and the arts. Naturally, we were thinking about ways to link these interests. Did he potentially want to be a reviewer or a critic? Or perhaps he'd like to curate evenings out featuring an elevated dinner followed by a theater experience.

One goal he stressed was "to have the impact to uplift other people." As he elaborated, "If I can make a difference, it's hopefully to help bring other people's art to life." Exploring these aspirations helped set off David's big bang. Two-thirds of the way through day two, I asked him, "If you could do absolutely anything and I could wave the magic wand and guarantee you success, what would you do?"

He swallowed hard and replied, "Okay, I don't know how it would ever work, but my dream is to be a Broadway producer."

I could tell this was a real dream because immediately came the "why nots." Down we delved into his field of resistance. In what ways did he feel inadequate or just clueless? "I don't even know how to find a contact to get me started," he protested. "Plus, I have no idea how to be a producer." Next followed, "I don't know how or where I'd raise the cash—I'm good at governance, not at asking for money." To which we opened new lines of questioning: "Help us outline the elements you need in order to do this. Tell us in detail why you think you can't do it, and then let's rebut those assumptions."

Thinking back on it now, David says:

> One of many things that I found so valuable about
> those couple of days was getting past what I'd call
> "lawyering to death" my ideas. A lawyer's job is to
> spot pitfalls and deal with them. Looking towards
> retirement, you think to yourself, I'd like to be an
> XYZ, but it takes a lot of time, it's expensive, and
> I don't know how to do it. You think of twenty
> reasons why it's problematic, and then you turn on
> the TV and forget it.

A turning point for David came with a bit of reframing we
proposed. Take the fundraising part, for example, which he found
particularly intimidating. He *hated* the idea of asking people for
money. "You're not asking people for money," we explained. "You're
actually making them aware of an opportunity—an opportunity
with limited availability that plenty of people would leap at if they
only knew it existed. Your role is to educate people about an opportunity—nothing more." The logic spoke to him as he recalled his
own quests for great Broadway shows to invest in. He had always
felt lucky to have gotten in on the chance when the right thing
came along.

We pressed on: "Who do you know who has raised money for
theater or even other causes? What can you learn from their methods
and pitches? And what do you need to learn about being a producer?"
In David's words:

> Before long, I had talked myself into realizing that
> I could probably do it. I made a chart of people
> I would like to talk to and what it would take to
> go about it all. And I read books and talked with
> people I knew.

Fast forward to 2019: David is onstage at the Tony Awards, where the latest musical he helped produce, *Hadestown,* has swept eight of its fourteen nominations, including Best Musical and Best Original Score. After less than two years in retirement, here was David with the rest of the *Hadestown* family, holding a Tony Award in his hand, pinching himself to check if this could actually be happening. He had achieved his audacious goal of becoming a Broadway producer, with a Tony award as icing on the cake! How fitting that the show, which updates the ancient Greek myths of Orpheus; Eurydice; King Hades; and his wife, Persephone, also pits faith against doubt and love against fear.

But let's back up to the start of this adventure. David had begun reaching into his network, exactly as we had suggested. He was simply asking for advice, gathering information, and really letting the world know what he wanted to be doing more of. It was the start of penetrating a new community, putting himself in the way of auspicious opportunities.

His first break came when a friend who knew of his aspiration to be a producer invited David to help produce a one-man Broadway show called *The Encounter.* The erstwhile lawyer kept an open mind, even as he doubted his credibility in the role. "My friend told me, 'You can come to the meetings and be at the table,'" David recalls. "I chalked it up as my tuition payment. It was how I learned about production, and it was the start of meeting theater people in the right ecosystem. It gave me an in."

The Encounter had a short but critically acclaimed run in 2016. Once it closed, David was back to networking again. Before long, a question came up over lunch with the executive director of the nonprofit theater company where David served on the board. A promising new musical was coming to Broadway, and he wanted to know if raising money for that show would constitute a conflict of interest. "No, it would not," David opined, and, in fact, he himself would be happy "to help fill the gap" in fundraising, as a producer. That production was *Hadestown.*

At the time of this writing, David has helped produce numerous shows, including *The Lightning Thief*; *Diana: the Musical*; *Good Night, Oscar*; *Once Upon a One More Time*; *The Cottage*; and *Water for Elephants*. David has become an active Broadway producer with a long and energizing runway ahead of him. Not only did the substance of his work go from black and white to color, but the people he works with also bring fresh sizzle to his life. He has cultivated a fabulous new community of theater friends in New York and Chicago, which has enriched his existence enormously.

I love David's story because it shines the light on pathfinding in a most dramatic way. Here's someone who had an "unlived life" and could not imagine how he would get from the legal business to show business. But he did it one step at a time. Had he allowed his doubting mind to run the show at the beginning, it would have been curtains (so to speak) for his big dream. The key takeaway? Don't kill the dream before it has a chance to come alive. Instead, treat it like a grand experiment.

The Experimental Mindset

When nurturing a new aspiration into existence, an experimental mindset offers a powerful antidote to the overly critical (and often stifling) mind. Because most of our clients have been paid to "get it right" throughout their careers, the value of experimentation may not be obvious to them. We take a moment to suggest that they approach the pathway to a new endeavor just like a scientist would approach a hypothesis—by conducting a series of experiments. We remind them that experiments do not succeed or fail—they merely provide us with data.

When we refer to an experimental mindset, we mean an approach characterized by curiosity, a willingness to take risks, and a focus on learning through trial and error. By turning an intimidating goal into an intelligent quest, the process itself becomes more important than any specific outcome. The following benefits of cultivating an experimental mindset can be game changers.

Adaptability: An experimental mindset encourages us to embrace uncertainty and change. We are more likely to adapt to new situations and challenges because we view them as opportunities for learning and growth.

Innovation and creativity: Experimentation is at the heart of innovation. With an experimental mindset, we are more likely to explore new ideas, think creatively, and come up with innovative solutions. We are not afraid to question the status quo and try unconventional approaches.

Continuous learning: Experimentation involves a continuous process of learning and refinement. We see every experience, whether success or failure, as an opportunity to gather insights and improve.

Risk-taking: A willingness to take calculated risks is a key component of an experimental mindset, reminding us that some level of risk is necessary for progress and enabling us to step outside our comfort zones to explore new possibilities.

Problem-solving: Experimentation is part of effective problem-solving. Instead of being deterred by challenges, we view problems as puzzles to be solved. We experiment with different approaches until we find solutions that work.

Resilience: Embracing an experimental mindset builds resilience. We become better equipped to handle setbacks and failures because we see them as integral parts of a learning process.

Flexibility: An experimental mindset fosters flexibility in thinking. We become more open to adjusting strategies based on feedback and results. This flexibility is crucial in dynamic environments where rigid approaches may not be effective.

Entrepreneurial spirit: Entrepreneurs often embody an experimental mindset. Starting and growing something new involves a continuous cycle of testing hypotheses, adapting to feedback, and refining strategies based on real-world results.

Armed with a new attitude, our clients can often set down the worrisome question of whether they will succeed at some specific thing and simply enjoy the experience of living (and experimenting) their way to the answer.

David Shapiro's observations five years into his retirement high-light the value of experimentation. While he ultimately achieved his big goal of becoming a producer, he developed a whole array of possible ideas for himself to experiment with, recognizing the theater pathway might only take him so far. In reviewing his original list of ideas, he muses:

> Now that I'm five years into it, I look at that list and have to redefine it. Because some of the things on that list are like, really? Why was that on the list? For example, since I was in college, I thought I'd really love to learn how to fly a plane but had neither the time nor the money. Suddenly, I had both but wondered whether the payback would be worth it. Probably not. So, I crossed it off the list. But there were some things on the list that I tried, such as taking tap dancing lessons. It was good exercise and tremendous fun, although no amount of time or effort would bring an old man like me to tap dance at any reasonable level.

The data was in: David was not going to become a professional tap dancer, but it was a fun experiment that offered him the chance to meet some new people and engage with a completely different challenge. Did he somehow view the tap dancing lessons as a mistake because he did not continue them indefinitely? Not in the slightest. He observes, "It begs the question: Is it the process itself that is the reward?" In our view, yes. The magic of life hides in our willingness to take action.

Action Planning

One of the most important documents we help our clients draft is an action plan. Getting into action is fundamental to moving forward. It is the start of building the bridge from where they are to where they want to be. It is the moment to push the boat into the river, so to speak.

We start by surveying both personal and professional realms and ask the following: "If you will have made real progress in the next thirty-, sixty-, and ninety-day periods, what will you have done?" By breaking the list down into these short-, medium-, and longer-term segments, we can help our clients see immediate opportunities for action but also plan for broader projects that will take longer to achieve, setting the stage for the inevitable iteration that will come.

We encourage our clients to focus on discrete actions in the short run while capturing desired outcomes in the longer run. Action items are things that can be checked off a list with a single step, whereas outcomes are more like projects, which contain a series of related action items. For example, a typical desired outcome is "update the trust and estate plan, now that the kids are grown." This is a great outcome to focus on, but it is not a single action item. Following up, we will ask for the next specific action that must be taken to move toward this outcome. "Oh, I need to call my lawyer and make an appointment for us to come in and review our new plan." Perfect— the call to the lawyer drops into the thirty-day action items, and we note the outcome "T&E Plan Updated" as a ninety-day goal.

We also prompt our clients to identify new habits that will help them experiment with shaping new life structures. James, a hard-charging CEO, comes to mind. He found himself caught in the years-long routine of staying in the office until at least eight p.m. every night, meaning he missed dinner with his spouse, Martha, who preferred to eat earlier than nine p.m. James had also revealed to us a love of cooking that he had developed as a young man, before his career had made it difficult to engage in that particular activity.

Yet James was now only six months away from his retirement date and still found it impossible to pull himself away from work in the evenings.

"How about trying this idea as an experiment?" we offered. "What if you start planning to leave the office at five-thirty p.m. just one day per week? On your walk home, hit the market for dinner ingredients and cook dinner for Martha."

James's enthusiasm for this idea was palpable, and we captured it as part of his thirty-day action plan. He would leave the office at five-thirty p.m. on the next Wednesday, having planned a menu for that night's dinner. The goal would be to repeat this each week during the next month with the longer-range idea being to expand it to another weekday as his runway toward retirement shortened.

It turned out to be just the commitment he needed to begin reshaping the end of his workday and disrupting the habit he had of working until eight p.m. By defining an appealing action to substitute for his existing habit of working late, James began living his way to a new routine that activated a latent creative interest and had the additional benefit of allowing him to spend meaningful time with Martha.

We also look for action items that can be delegated to others. Often, a jumble of administrative tasks accompanies the process of retiring (more on this in chapter 12), and the mere act of capturing them begins to loosen the paralysis caused by too many unanchored and ill-defined chores. An example involves understanding how health insurance will work. Our clients, used to tackling thorny problems on their own, forget that they likely have resources available to sort through some of these questions. The next action, then, is merely a delegation. "Can we delegate to your assistant the task of asking the HR department for an overview of how health insurance will work after you retire?"

"Why didn't I think of that? Of course."

"Great—once you have more information, you can decide what the next action item is to nail this down."

The more challenging action items to define are often those linked to the new ideas for engagement that we have identified. But we remind our clients that, in six months, they will wish they had started now. Focused as we are on initial activities tied to information gathering and networking, we ask what specific research tasks occur to them (can they be delegated?) and who they would like to connect with about their idea. Who can offer advice? Is that person local, so an in-person meeting would be possible, or is it more practical to think about a video conference because they are in another city? Once clarified, these discrete action items land on the action plan. As a rejoinder, we remind them that the results of their research and conversation will generate new sparks for new actions. So, there is no need to get overly concerned about what happens next. Like a hike up a mountain, it is the next step in the right direction that ultimately takes you to the top.

Visual Example of Action Plan

Item	Action Required	Priority	30/60/90	Notes	Status
Advice from John B.	Call and set coffee	High	30	Discuss experience self-publishng	Complete
Find a personal trainer	Research trainers in my area; ask for recommendations from friends	High	30	Need someone to come to my home gym	In Progress
Update trust and estate plan	Call lawyer	Medium	60	Get information on retiement benefits first	Not Started

Part of our action-planning framework assumes an ongoing consultative coaching relationship with our clients. For one thing, we serve as accountability partners. Almost without fail, our still-busy clients tell us that the first post-session meeting with us spurred them into a flurry of action—even on those items that caused them the greatest discomfort. Keying off of a common value of responsibility, it is a rare client who will blow off a commitment made to a third party (in this case, us). Accountability, then, can provide invaluable fuel in the early days, when the combination of inertia and uncertainty can stoke self-doubt.

With fifteen years of experience to back us up, we are strong believers that a coach can be the difference between making bold progress and giving in to the natural resistance that can sideline any great goal. A fair number of our clients bristle at the term *coach* and wonder what such a person could possibly offer them—that is, until they work with one and realize this: we humans are often the thing standing in the way of our next great endeavor. A good coach helps us get out of the way of what wants to happen.

Slow and Steady . . .

As is probably clear by now, I like to chuckle at myself as often as possible. Frequently, my musings about my own personality traits resonate with our clients who have also typically been driven for most of their lives. They've pushed themselves hard and to great effect. Intensity is a familiar friend.

Maybe four years into my legal career, a colleague and close friend left an amusing magnet on my desk. On it was depicted a wild-eyed guy at his desk surrounded by mountains of coffee cups. The caption read, "Slow and steady gets me nowhere." At the time, it described me perfectly: revved to the max, quick to expect results, and impatient as hell. I laughed my head off at the implication, feeling gleeful that someone had noticed my fabulous intensity. (The magnet is still on my desk, by the way).

Add to my Type A personality a certain conditioning that we all experience, which I call the montage effect. The movie montage, pioneered by Soviet filmmaker Sergei Eisenstein, is a filmmaking technique used to create the illusion of the passage of time, allowing filmmakers to cover weeks, months, and even years in the pursuit of a long-range outcome. It's that glorious two minutes in a movie when we watch our beleaguered protagonist go from loser to winner, from an out-of-shape weakling to an unbeatable champion. What a delicious sense of triumph!

These days, this phenomenon is only exacerbated by the on-slaught of social and traditional media highlight reels, where it looks like everyone leaps from peak to peak, somehow deftly side-stepping even a hint of struggle or failure along the way. We seem to enter each narrative at an opportune moment when everything is going right. No one wants to tell the story from the middle of a hopeless slog.

For these reasons, when I embarked on my post–big law life adventure, I expected everything I tried to do to materialize im-mediately, as if my penetrating focus was enough to manifest a real-life montage of instant success. Of course, over time, I learned to drop the panicky need to rush to an ideal outcome and to stop taking score too soon. Because, as it turns out, slow and steady got me everywhere.

As our clients prepare to get into action, we emphasize the value of incremental progress and the accompanying need for patience. There is simply no rush, and great outcomes take time.

One common fallacy our clients sometimes nurse: "If I'm out of the game for three months, I'm done! I'm toast!" It falls to us to dispel their fears. "Just because you haven't found the situation that you're looking for yet doesn't mean it's never going to happen," we'll remind them. "It's not like when you're twenty-five, and you can't have a three-month gap on your resume. You are going to be fine." In fact, sometimes, we actually encourage the notion of a year-long sabbatical as a way to recalibrate before getting too deeply involved in another commitment. We have never seen this approach sideline a client when they later decided it was time to get involved again.

Never was patience more crucial than for those of our clients who retired during the 2020 pandemic. Mark, a successful investment banker, comes to mind. In February 2020, he snagged us for a planning session. Mark was fifty-nine, and it was culturally time for him to retire from his firm. While he understood that, he still wanted to work for another five to seven years in a paid position. He simply wasn't ready to be done.

As someone who developed Type 1 diabetes in his twenties, Mark had become extremely knowledgeable about the medical field, even while still in the heart of his career. His approach to navigating diabetes had included studying his disease so deeply that he often found himself as knowledgeable as his own doctors. Mark had an impressive capacity for absorbing and synthesizing complex information and still found the medical field fascinating. With his interests and skill set, a position with a biotech firm would suit him to a tee. That was the conclusion of our two-day interaction, and Mark felt energized by the idea and was set to begin his research and networking campaigns.

So much for timing. Two weeks later, COVID-19 lockdowns rolled out across the United States. The plans we laid out in our session would go frustratingly dormant. Trying to make the best of it, we provided virtual coaching for another six months. Yet with the pandemic in full swing, Mark found it too tough to make progress; the whole world was in shell shock and withdrawal. We agreed it made sense to put his efforts on hold until things opened up again. And we reassured Mark that the world would be just as interested in what he had to offer then as it would have been the day he retired.

To Mark's credit, as soon as the vaccines rolled out and a sense of hope returned to the planet, he refreshed his research into possible biotech opportunities and set up Zoom meetings with relevant connections. He faithfully engaged the process, progressively seeking advice and asking for new introductions, just as we had advised.

By mid-2022, Mark was reaching out with cheery news. He had just been offered the position of strategic advisor for a venture capital fund that invests in biotech start-ups. He needed our feedback on his professional bio.

We raised glasses to him across the Zoom screen, acknowledging the fortitude it had taken to make this happen in the face of a global pandemic. Mark had come through his quest with the job of his dreams. With a pandemic to slog through, no doubt it took longer than it might have. But finding the right opportunity requires steady and consistent effort, whether it's a paying job or an unpaid engagement. We remind our clients they should not become demoralized if things don't materialize right away. There is a method to smoking out opportunities, and steady effort and incremental progress are part of that method.

Building and Maintaining Momentum

In physics, momentum is a fundamental concept that describes the quantity of motion an object possesses. It is a vector quantity, meaning it has both magnitude and direction. In everyday language, momentum is often used metaphorically to describe the strength or force gained by something, such as a project, idea, or movement. The term conveys the idea of building and sustaining energy over time, regardless of the natural resistance encountered.

Recognizing that, like gravity, resistance and obstacles are part of the deal, we counsel our clients to expect challenges to appear as they get into action. It is for this reason that momentum is so critical. Momentum keeps you in the boat. We emphasize four helpful strategies:

1. **Realistic optimism** is the most useful attitude to have when embarking on something new. Grounded in positive expectations, this mindset helps avoid the "why bother?" goblin that can rear its head at the first sign of struggle. By assuming an optimistic outlook while at the same time

anticipating challenges, we can prime ourselves for curiosity, creative problem-solving, and iterative thinking. When the obstacles appear, no problem—we knew they were coming, and we are reminded our job is to maintain momentum regardless. As Dr. Alex Lickerman puts it in his wonderful book, *The Undefeated Mind: On the Science of Constructing an Indestructible Self*: "The reason optimism yields results isn't that we necessarily tend to try harder when we think a goal is achievable; rather, we tend to try more often." That is momentum.

2. **Relaxed determination** is the bearing we find most helpful to our clients. After all, every one of them has an array of impressive accomplishments. They've already checked the success box. Finally, there is an opportunity to approach the next ambition with a sense of internal calm—is success or failure really the relevant standard at this point? Is it possible to relax into the thought that the journey ahead will be rich and rewarding, regardless of where it goes? At the same time, we suggest to our clients that they retain the same fierce determination they've always used to get things done. The force of will is a powerful thing. As one of our clients put it, "Take it easy, but take it."

3. **Emphasizing every win** is a way of focusing the mind on the encouraging data points accumulating along the way. Our brains are wired to focus on negative inputs, even when those negative inputs are miniscule. An example from my own experience highlights this phenomenon. As a person who enjoys public speaking, I was delighted when I was asked to give the commencement address at a local high school a few years ago. Of course, I relished having this new experience, but I also brought a degree of jitters along with me as I stared into the faces of the senior class—all of whom were almost certainly hoping I'd keep my remarks short. I picked up on one face in the audience that seemed

disengaged or, worse, bored stiff by my presentation. Despite the rousing applause when I concluded, I could not get that one impression out of my mind. Trying to sleep that night, I had largely decided I should never accept such an invitation again, considering what a disaster the whole thing had probably been. The next day, I received no fewer than seven inquiries from attendees for a copy of my remarks, which they said had inspired them. And I was reminded how easily we can let one negative input overshadow a thoroughly positive experience.

4. **Staying in action** is everything. There is always a next action available, and sometimes that next action is simply hidden inside of a larger and overwhelming project. The key is to break that project down further until there is a clear and accessible action to take. It might be a call to a knowledgeable person for advice or a piece of research or a request for help from an expert. When momentum is threatened by an imposing obstacle, identifying and then having the courage to take the next small action can be the difference between pushing through and packing it in. As I often remind myself in moments of paralysis, if I could think myself out of my predicament, I would have done it by now. Enough ruminating—it's time to act.

Enjoying the Ride

And here we come to the most important piece of advice we could ever offer to anyone on the brink of an uncertainty, such as retirement. Whatever your next ride is to be, insist on enjoying it because it will not go on forever.

I want to unpack this word *enjoy* because I do not mean to suggest merely experiencing fun or pleasure. Not that there is anything wrong with those things, but I am referring to a deeper sense of meaning and satisfaction that comes from rejoicing in the opportunity to be precisely where you are, doing what you are doing. I recently read Oliver Burkeman's fabulous book *Four Thousand Weeks: Time Management for Mortals.* His opening line grabs one's attention as a stark reminder of what we all busy ourselves trying to forget: "The average human lifespan is absurdly, terrifyingly, insultingly short." He goes on to highlight the scientific consensus that humans likely appeared some two hundred thousand years ago, but assuming we live to eighty, we will have been granted just four thousand weeks of life. Considering our relatively miniscule space on this time continuum, Burkeman reminds us via a quote from Thomas Nagel, "[W]e will all be dead any minute."

Is this a depressing reminder? Not at all—just the opposite. It is an enchanting invitation to grab life by the shirt collar and go for it. If not now, then when? What else must click into place, we ask our clients, before you give yourself permission to take a big, juicy, possibly messy bite out of life just for the sheer enjoyment of adventure and discovery? And perhaps the single most important metric of success in this next chapter is whether there is an abundance of enjoyment, appreciation, contribution, and generosity. These are the attributes our most content clients reflect back to us after they have constructed a new version of life for themselves. What, really, have you got to lose?

I keep a Latin phrase, *Serius est quam cogitas,* taped inside my morning journal as a reminder that I have no time to waste standing on the shore worrying about what will happen on the river. Translation? It's later than you think.

The ride awaits.

Chapter Summary

Although pursuing a big dream can feel intimidating, don't kill it out of fear before it ever has a chance.

Rather than needing to know whether ideas will succeed or fail, treat them as experiments that permit the accumulation of data, which will then permit the opportunity to make adjustments, carry on, or pursue something altogether different.

Getting into action is the key to moving from idea to reality. Looking for the next small action to take can get things moving when paralysis sets in. Working with a coach can often provide much-needed accountability to push on.

Recognize that slow and steady progress is both adequate and realistic. Each step in the right direction takes us closer to our goals. Life is not a montage. Don't take score too soon.

Prioritize the process over any specific outcome, allowing momentum to indicate progress and serve as the answer to obstacles and resistance.

Above all, enjoy the ride. You have worked hard, and it is later than you think.

chapter twelve

TACKLING THE PRACTICAL STUFF: A SIX-MONTH CHECKLIST

Opportunity is a haughty goddess who wastes no time with those who are unprepared.

~ George S. Clason, author

The Power of Going Public

O ur clients tend to come to us in one of three situations: (1) they know the date they will retire, but almost no one else does; (2) they have a possible target date in mind, but they need help vetting it; or (3) they are still several years away from retiring, but they are proactive planners by nature, and they want to be intentional about how they approach the entire enterprise.

From our perspective, there is a critical difference between setting a target date in one's own mind and going public with that date. Both these decisions require careful consideration and are heavily influenced by the specific circumstances of the person retiring. As the material in this book has hopefully made clear, it is almost never too early to begin planning privately for life after retirement. Notably, the evolution of one's identity is more approachable over time, and some future goals benefit enormously from a years-long investment. When to go public with a retirement date, however, must be meticulously thought through. An overly early announcement can create a premature sense of irrelevance or even negatively affect compensation. Leaving the announcement too late, though, is equally ill advised.

The pros of announcing one's retirement can include:

- Opportunity to network with colleagues, clients, and others regarding future endeavors
- Time for psychological adjustment
- An adequate runway for succession planning
- Access to resources in one's organization
- Latitude to complete any unfinished legacy projects
- Service as a proactive retirement role model in your organization

The risks of announcing one's retirement too soon can include:

- Reduced compensation or equity
- Curtailed involvement in new client matters or firm/company projects
- Arousal of client concerns about the team's ability to handle ongoing matters
- A sense of limbo over an extended period

As a general rule, eighteen months out seems to be a solid runway in terms of confirming your retirement date to yourself, and a year out is generally about right to begin spreading the word, at least internally within your firm or company.

While timing for discussions with clients can vary, as I noted in chapter 9, clients want to be informed as early in the process as possible so there's plenty of time to settle any concerns about the team that's taking over. Your continued presence for a generous period of time provides you the opportunity to step back gradually and allow clients to adjust to your diminishing role in a measured way. Perhaps even more importantly, announcing your planned retirement frees you up to start consulting with your network about the future. If you're keeping your retirement a secret, you can't talk to anybody, get advice, or network about your ideas. You're essentially disabling the power of your strategic connections and resources by hiding the fact that you're going to retire, which serves no one. Instead, we recommend using your retirement conversations to introduce your ideas for future engagement, ask for advice, and seek introductions to others who might have information or relevant connections.

Shaping the Final Six Months

Beyond the psychological and lifestyle adjustments associated with retirement, there are a myriad of practical items that must be addressed, and they take time. I have mentioned most of them throughout this book, but below is a concise six-month checklist of questions and action items that captures the most common practical issues facing you when you retire. Handling them in an organized and proactive way is key to an empowered and smooth transition into retirement.

Succession Planning Fundamentals

While, ideally, the critical aspects of true succession planning have been happening for years (building a talent pipeline and including younger team members in key matters), the following action items and questions can provide a guide for how to think more specifically about making sure your team and your clients (or customers, patients, etc., as applicable) are "tucked in" before you retire.

- Create an inventory of your clients, including their key contacts, ongoing matters, and current team members involved.
- Create an inventory of your pending administrative responsibilities (committees, projects, ongoing initiatives) within the organization that will require a successor.
- Create an inventory of your external community or marketing roles that will require a successor, including board positions, regular speaking engagements, conferences, and other relevant events you have regularly attended as part of your overall professional life.
- Ensure you have identified potential candidates to inherit each of the above clients, matters, and roles and be prepared to discuss their succession with the appropriate internal people, including leadership, other team members, and the potential successors themselves.
- If no clear succession candidate exists, ensure that leadership understands the potential gap and is equipped to address it, where possible.

Questions to ask and answer:

- What is the optimal timing to discuss your retirement and succession with each client? Will you have this discussion in person, over a video call, or by phone?
- Are you prepared to discuss any fresh endeavors of your own so you can begin to solicit advice and introductions where relevant?
- If there are clients for whom in-person conversations are important, have you mapped out the schedule of travel that will allow them adequate advance notice?

- Where you have a client base that is interconnected, be sure to have these conversations in a thoughtful order and on a confidential basis so each client hears your news from you and not others.
- Have you brought those colleagues who will succeed you into the relevant external conversations? Have you solicited their viewpoints on any transition concerns?
- Do you have adequate time to conclude any legacy projects that are important to you?
- Have you established a way to transfer critical knowledge, tools, and institutional or client history to your successors?
- Everyone will ask "What are you going to be doing next?" Be prepared with your answer, even if it is only a placeholder for now.

Financial Matters

The majority of our clients have robust financial planning and management resources available to them. Nevertheless, the inflection point of retirement provides an opportune moment to reexamine various items associated with personal finance.

- Do you (and your partner, if applicable) have adequate visibility into monthly and annual expenditures that you (both) feel confident about regarding spending patterns and ongoing lifestyle choices?
- Have you identified purpose-driven "permission budgets" for various areas of planned spending (like travel, familial support, or charitable giving) and asked your financial planner to model those budgets into your overall plan?
- Have you reviewed a cash flow and overall withdrawal strategy with your financial adviser?
- Are your trust and estate planning documents up to date?

- Do your various insurance policies still make sense, and if not, what opportunities exist to reshape them?
- What is your plan for health insurance? Will your organization continue to provide coverage until you qualify for Medicare? Will you want or need a supplemental policy at that time?
- Have you determined the right time to apply for Social Security benefits?

Organizational Policies and Procedures

Because retirement is roundly avoided as a topic of discussion in many organizations, we frequently discover that our clients have almost no idea of the resources, benefits, policies, and procedures that accompany retiring from their organizations. We recommend considering the following questions.

- Is there a department or individual in the organization who handles retirement functions? If so, contact them and request a detailed rundown of all relevant resources, benefits, policies, and procedures.
- Does the organization offer outside resources relating to items such as health insurance, long-term care insurance, or other forms of insurance?
- If your organization offers a retirement benefit, do you understand how it works? Does your financial manager have all the relevant information to guide you?
- Will you be able to keep your desktop, laptop, cell phone, or other equipment?
- What will happen to your email address?
- Are there alumni benefits that might be helpful to you, such as the occasional use of an office or conference room?

- Is there an alumni network in your organization that you want to stay engaged with?
- Will your bio stay on the organization's website for a period of time? Will they forward any emails or calls that come to you?
- Does your organization provide research or networking support as you explore new possibilities or endeavors?

Digital Transition

So much of our lives is now lived in the digital realm, and most of our clients have conducted their personal lives largely in the context of their professional worlds, including paper file storage, digital file storage, email communications, contacts, and repeating calendar notations. Drilling down on the specifics of what we call your digital transition is absolutely crucial. It takes time and usually assistance from your technology team. Make sure you have asked and addressed the following questions, as applicable:

- Do you have a personal email address you will be using in retirement? If not, would you prefer a new professional email address that ties to a new endeavor, or will you be using a common email platform, such as Gmail or Outlook?
- Have you used your current professional email address to log into accounts of any type or in connection with things like Global Entry or TSA Precheck? If so, now is the time to begin revising your usernames across the board. If you neglect to take this step, and your professional email ceases to exist, you will inevitably find yourself locked out of accounts and websites over time. We have heard these horror stories, and they are to be avoided!

- Are there personal emails or papers stored on your computer or in the organization's virtual file system that you will need to transfer to a new filing environment?
- Are there repeating calendar entries (such as birthdays, appointments, or other personal reminders) that you would like to transfer to a new calendar environment?
- Have you arranged to export your contacts into your new digital environment?
- Are there software licenses you will need or want to purchase for use in your home environment?
- Do you have the required tech support to implement new technology solutions for your home office environment? Do you have a tech support resource for ongoing maintenance and data security?

Expressing Appreciation and Gratitude

- As your final six months begin to wind down, pay attention to the "lasts" as they occur. For example, you might be attending your last partners' meeting, conducting your last performance reviews, or holding your last meetings with mentees. It is worth noticing your final experience of these moments and appreciating them.
- Consider whom in your organization you would like to thank for their support along the way, including staff and administrative personnel. They have often been the unsung heroes who have made your job easier and more enjoyable. Whether you acknowledge them individually with a note and a gift or as a group with a lunch outing or an office event, this opportunity to express gratitude can produce meaningful and memorable moments for you as well as those you thank.

Planning a Celebration and Saying Goodbye

- Consider whether you will host a celebration to commemorate your retirement and, if so, to what extent you will include colleagues. These sorts of events offer those around you an opportunity to express admiration for your accomplishments and contributions. If colleagues are involved, such events also provide a common space for them to say their goodbyes and express their best wishes for you.

- We sometimes hear that retirement celebrations feel selfish or self-aggrandizing, but in our experience, they are an important form of closure for your colleagues. Bear this in mind as you decide whether and to what extent a celebration feels right. These celebrations can be just as meaningful after your official retirement, so if that timing works better for you, plan accordingly.

- Will you want to send a farewell message to your colleagues, partners, or team members? Many of our clients prepare wonderful farewell emails, some touching, some funny, and some a bit of both. These messages are widely enjoyed by those who receive them.

New Professional Identity

- If you are moving in a new professional direction, begin working on an updated CV, summary bio, and LinkedIn profile. At the time of this writing, unless you have a robust online biography with a new organization, the world expects to be able to find you on LinkedIn. Be sure to craft your materials so they speak to the future while incorporating your professional history.

- Determine whether you will want or need an email address that reflects a new professional role. For example, if you are considering consulting in a certain niche, you might want an email address that goes beyond @outlook.com or @ gmail.com.

- Along the same lines, determine whether you will need a website to align with your new activities or roles and begin working on this project at least three months before you want it to go live. Build in adequate lead time for any social media platforms you may wish to operate as well.

Base of Operations

- Will you need assistance physically moving out of your office? Can you accommodate office furnishings and personal items in your home office?
- Will you require office space outside the home or an upgrade to your home office?
- Will you need or want executive assistant support after you retire?
- Will you need or want specific help with other items that your employer routinely handled for you (such as tech support, travel, online security, registrations, and memberships)?
- If any of these items will be important to you, start resolving them well before your actual retirement date.

Planning Year One

- Once you know your retirement date, we heartily suggest purchasing an annual planning calendar on which you can begin mapping out the ensuing year. You will have a new level of control over your time and schedule, allowing you to proactively design the year ahead.

- Consider planning a special trip soon after you retire—one that would have been hard to justify or enjoy during your career. This trip might be the first time in decades you can leave your email inbox behind, and it can also serve as a wonderful way to "reset" yourself and your stress levels after you retire.
- Place yourself at the end of year one and ask yourself (and your spouse or partner) whom you would like to have seen, where you would like to have visited, and what projects you would like to have started or completed. Begin plotting these items out on your calendar. Putting shape to the first year can provide a sense of reassurance that you'll have plenty to do and also put you in the driver's seat of long-term planning.
- Most of all, look ahead with enthusiasm and anticipation. You are graduating into the next great chapter of your life.

I often get asked for practical tools to help with implementing some of the ideas in *Encore*. I am offering access to some of the most commonly requested tools as a free bonus. You can download them as described below.

Encore Bonus Materials

Networking Resources
(https://bit.ly/encorebonus1)
All opportunities are attached to people, and at this stage in your career, you have honed skills and developed a reputation that places you in great demand. Your job is to light up your network so that your connections, as well as connections of your connections, know that you are available and open to the right opportunities.

How to Use an Annual Planning Calendar?
(https://bit.ly/encorebonus2)
This exercise will help you prioritize the projects, trips, and events that are most important to you and help you determine what else you might have room for along the way. Once you've established the overview of your year, you can transfer your plans into your digital calendar.

Stay Connected with Elizabeth

- **Connect on LinkedIn:** Follow Elizabeth Zelinka Parsons for updates, insights, and professional connections.
- **Listen to Podcast Interviews:** Dive into topics of career transitions, high achievement, and thriving in retirement. Visit www.encoraco.com/medial
- **Get in Touch:** Have questions or want to connect further? Visit: www.encoraco.com/contact-us for inquiries.

ACKNOWLEDGMENTS

Where do I begin to acknowledge the wonderful people who have helped make this, my first book, possible? I must start with the hundreds of clients who have placed their trust in me and my husband and cofacilitator, David Parsons, to guide them through retirement and into their next chapters with confidence and enthusiasm. Without the insights that have emerged from their experiences and inspiring paths, there would be no book and nothing new for me to say about retirement. When I sought to solve this problem for myself two decades ago, I was groping in the dark for ways to rebuild my identity, my purpose—my entire life, really. Sharing my personal insights with our early clients allowed a deep and meaningful conversation to begin—one about intense careers, how to let go of them, and what it means to embrace whatever comes next. We have learned so much together.

I must next acknowledge with tremendous gratitude the five individuals who agreed to be profiled in this book: Peggy Davenport and Kirk Davenport, David Shapiro, Bob Wyman, and Ted Sonnenschein. They so willingly devoted their time to support this project and shared their stories openly so others could take whatever inspiration or insight they might need. I appreciate and applaud their generosity.

My chief professional collaborator, David Parsons, has been pivotal to helping me to shape the ideas, strategies, and tactics that appear throughout this book. Perhaps more a man of action than theory, his energy and drive have been without question part of what fueled my belief that this book could happen. Thank you to my trusted business partner and enduring friend for encouraging me in this project and for making these ideas better.

Laura Blum masterfully took me from concept to content as she skillfully questioned me and helped shape the stories and themes that are the backbone of this book. Her wonderful passages brought so much of the material to life in ways I could not have managed without her fabulous collaboration. Similarly, Laura Schaefer brought a sharp editor's eye to the structured manuscript, helping me make every recommendation more actionable, every insight more accessible. This book would still be a pile of notes without the talent and expertise of these two wonderful women.

I am eternally indebted to my many early-stage readers along the way, who offered comments and encouragement on what sometimes felt like a lonely and hopeless journey. They include Sonya Rudenstine, Paula Shoup, Janelle Crowell, Traci Riccitello, Molly Cassidy, and Kevin Poyck, my dear brother. Noby Mislang, my executive assistant, also offered me invaluable encouragement, support, and strategic advice as I began the daunting task of sharing my work with the world. She also designed the wonderful diagrams included throughout the book.

And finally, but always mostly: eternal gratitude to my amazing and lovely family: Mom—thanks for always believing in me, especially given my unique approach to life. David—your unfailing devotion is my terra firma—you know what I mean. Joe, Fin, Audrey, and Lucy—you surround me in joy and love. It will always be my greatest honor to have loved and been loved by each of you. And Stella, my darling dachshund, do not fear I've forgotten you. If writers can have copilots, you have been mine. Not a word of this book was written without you tucked up against me.

www.ingramcontent.com/pod-product-compliance
Lightning Source LLC
Chambersburg PA
CBHW060912120626
46553CB00001B/294